DK EYEWITNESS

T0276766

# TOP 10
# ANDALUCÍA
## AND THE COSTA DEL SOL

# Top 10 Andalucía and the Costa del Sol Highlights

# The Top 10 of Everything

# CONTENTS

## Andalucía and the Costa del Sol Area by Area

## Streetsmart

Within each Top 10 list in this book, no hierarchy of quality or popularity is implied. All 10 are, in the editor's opinion, of roughly equal merit.

***Title page, front cover and spine*** *The grand city of Málaga at sunset*
***Back cover, clockwise from top left*** *Spanish tapas; Roman bridge, Córdoba; Nerja beach; Cathedral at sunset, Málaga; Old Town, Málaga*

The rate at which the world is changing is constantly keeping the DK Eyewitness team on our toes. While we've worked hard to ensure that this edition of Andalucía and the Costa del Sol is accurate and up-to-date, we know that opening hours alter, standards shift, prices fluctuate, places close and new ones pop up in their stead. So, if you notice we've got something wrong or left something out, we want to hear about it. Please get in touch at **travelguides@dk.com**

# Welcome to
# Andalucía and the Costa del Sol

Flamenco, wine, tapas, beaches, sunshine: all the things that make Spain one of the best-loved and most visited countries on earth is concentrated in the region of Andalucía. But this beguiling region is also home to some of Europe's most romantic cities, its most important wetlands reserve and second-highest mountain range, offering a wealth of outdoor pursuits from hiking to skiing. With DK Eyewitness Top 10 Andalucía and the Costa del Sol, it's yours to explore.

Andalucía's three great cities – **Granada**, **Seville** and **Córdoba** – are repositories of Spain's historical identity and symbols of the area's Moorish past, with world-class heritage sites such as the **Mezquita** in Córdoba, Granada's **Alhambra** and Seville's **Cathedral**. Other must-sees are **Jerez de la Frontera** and its sherry *bodegas* and **Ronda**, with its location above the **Tajo** gorge, while **Baeza** and **Úbeda** are well-preserved towns full of Renaissance architecture. In between are the famous *pueblos blancos* (white villages) that dot the hilltops.

Along the sun-drenched **Costa del Sol**, cultural and culinary riches are concentrated around **Málaga**, **Marbella** and **Gibraltar**. Between the dramatic "rock" and the ancient city of **Cádiz** lies the gorgeous **Costa de la Luz**, popular with Spanish tourists and windsurfers.

Whether you're visiting for a weekend or a week, our Top 10 guide brings together the best of everything the region has to offer. The guide has useful tips throughout, from seeking out what's free to finding places off the beaten track, plus seven easy-to-follow itineraries, designed to tie together a clutch of sights in a short space of time. Add inspiring photography and detailed maps, and you've got the essential pocket-sized travel companion. **Enjoy the book**, and enjoy Andalucía and the Costa del Sol.

Clockwise from top: **The Alhambra, Granada**, Sierra de Aracena, Alcázar, Seville, Cabo de Gata nature reserve, Andalucían wall tiles, Ronda atop the Tajo gorge, La Mezquita, Córdoba

# Exploring Andalucía and the Costa del Sol

The region offers a dizzying range of sights, sounds, flavours and fun. To start you off, here are ideas for a four- and seven-day tour.

## Four Days in Andalucía

### Day ❶

**MORNING**

Follow the dramatic winding A397 up through the coastal mountains of the Serranías Penibéticas to lunch in **Ronda** *(see pp30–31)*. Take in the architecture of the bullring, palaces and the view from the Puente Nuevo.

**AFTERNOON**

Drive to **Cádiz** *(see pp26–7)* and wander the backstreets of the medieval Barrio del Pópulo; don't miss the Catedral Nueva and the coastal promenade.

### Day ❷

**MORNING**

Explore the **Parque Nacional Doñana** *(see pp36–7)*, catching the birdlife at dawn. Next visit **Jerez de la Frontera** *(see p106)* to sample the local sherries.

**AFTERNOON**

Enjoy the back-road route north via the *pueblo blanco* of **Arcos de la Frontera** *(see p106)* to **Seville** *(see pp84–93)* and its **Cathedral** and **La Giralda** *(see pp18–19)*.

### Day ❸

**MORNING**

Visit Seville's **Real Alcázar** *(see pp20–21)* before driving on to the white village of **Carmona** *(see p96)*, then on to **Córdoba** *(see pp22–3)*.

**AFTERNOON**

Tour **La Mezquita** *(see pp24–5)*, the **Judería** *(see p22)* and the **Alcázar de los Reyes Cristianos** *(see p23)*.

**The Catedral Nueva** sits proudly above Cádiz seafront.

**Sierra de Cazorla** is a vast and diverse reserve.

**The impressive Alhambra** is a complex of Moorish fortresses and gardens.

**Key**
— Four-day itinerary
— Seven-day itinerary

**Arcos de la Frontera** is dramatically situated on a cliff edge.

### Day ❹
Head to **Granada** (see pp116–123) to see the architectural complex and gardens of **the Alhambra** (see pp12–13) and **Generalife** (summer palace) (see pp14–15), then finally relax on the beach at **Nerja** (see p33).

## Seven Days in Andalucía

### Days ❶–❸ as above
### Day ❹
Start at **the Alhambra** (see pp12–13), then explore the **Albaicín** quarter (see pp16–17), taking in the churches, Moorish baths and Moroccan tearooms. Afterwards, visit UNESCO-listed **Úbeda's Pottery Quarter** (see p35), pretty plazas and Renaissance and Plateresque buildings.

### Day ❺
Go for a short hike in the **Sierra de Cazorla** (see p61) and look out for birds of prey. Spend the afternoon in beautifully preserved **Baeza** (see p34), another UNESCO-listed site.

### Day ❻
Discover the **Sierra Nevada** (see pp38–9), Europe's second-highest mountain range after the Alps. If it's summer, see the Valle de Lecrín's olive, almond and citrus groves; in winter, you can go skiing.

### Day ❼
Take the A41 south, along the western edge of the **Sierra Nevada** (see pp38–9) and enjoy the beach at Nerja before visiting the market town of Vélez-Málaga on **the Costa del Sol** (see pp32–3).

# Top 10 Andalucía and the Costa del Sol Highlights

The impressive Puente Nuevo spans El Tajo gorge at Ronda

# TOP10 Andalucía Highlights

The autonomous region of Andalucía dominates southern Spain, with its dramatic landscape of deserts, olive groves and snowcapped mountains. Memories of a visit here will be colourful, joyous and deeply stirring, and will likely include flamenco, remote white villages, sierras and sunny beaches.

### ① Moorish Granada
Andalucía's 1,300-year-old Moorish heritage evokes pure Romanticism that is hard to equal. The delicate art and architecture are among the most splendid in Europe (see pp12–17).

### ② Seville Cathedral and La Giralda
These two chief wonders of Seville beautifully embody the juxtaposition of the Moors and their Christian successors (see pp18–19).

### Real Alcázar, Seville ③

A mix of styles is evident in this luxurious palace, mostly built by Moorish artisans for Christians (see pp20–21).

### ④ Córdoba and La Mezquita
This was once the most important Islamic city in Europe, a fact that is illustrated by the architectural masterpiece of La Mezquita, the Great Mosque (see pp22–5).

### Cádiz ⑤

Said to be Europe's oldest constantly inhabited city, Cádiz retains a mysterious aura. Its golden-domed cathedral is spectacular (see pp26–7).

0 kilometres 50
0 miles 50

Jabugo  Aracena  Cazalla de la Sierra
Minas de Riotinto  Lora del Río
**HUELVA**  ② ③
Gibraleón  Seville • Alcalá de Guadaira
Huelva  **SEVILLA**
Parque Nacional de Doñana ⑨
Arcos de la Frontera
Jerez de la Frontera  **CÁDIZ**
Cádiz ⑤  San Fernando
Costa de la Luz  Algeciras

**6** **Ronda**
The largest of the *pueblos blancos* scattered throughout the region, Ronda is split by El Tajo gorge. It is also reputed to be the birthplace of the modern style of bullfighting (see pp30–31).

**The Costa del Sol** **7**
From the wealthy yachting-set enclaves to package deals for families, this famous expanse of sand has something for everyone (see pp32–3).

**Baeza and Úbeda** **8**
Both of these exquisite towns in Jaén Province offer world-class Renaissance architecture set in perfectly preserved historic centres (see pp34–5).

**9** **Parque Nacional de Doñana**
The vast delta of the Guadalquivir River is one of the world's most vital nature reserves; without it birdlife throughout Europe would be seriously compromised (see pp36–7).

**The Sierra Nevada** **10**
Europe's second-highest mountain range after the Alps offers its southernmost ski resort, a wealth of wildlife for trekkers, and dozens of remote traditional villages along its southern slopes (see pp38–9).

# TOP 10 ⭐ Moorish Granada: the Alhambra

The great complex of the Alhambra is the best-preserved medieval Arab palace in the world and, with nearly two million visitors annually, it is also the most popular monument in Spain. Built on the Sabika Hill overlooking the city of Granada, its most distinctive phase began in the 11th century as the *qa'lat al-Hamra* (Red Fort) of the Ziridian rulers. From the 13th to almost the end of the 15th century the kings of the succeeding Nasrid dynasty embellished the site in a most spectacular fashion.

**1 Puerta de la Justicia**

Built in 1348, the "Justice Gate" **(above)** horseshoe arch makes use of Arab defensive techniques – a steep approach combined with four right-angled turns – intended to slow down invading armies.

The Alhambra, backed by the Sierra Nevada

**2 Puerta del Vino**

The "Wine Gate" – so called because it was used as a wine cellar in the 16th century – marks what was once the main entrance arch to the Medina (market).

**3 Plaza de los Aljibes**

From these ramparts, visitors can enjoy superb views of Granada. The giant cisterns *(aljibes)* underneath were built by the Christian successors.

**4 Alcazaba**

Although largely in ruins, this fortress is well worth a look. Don't miss climbing up onto the Torre de la Vela for views of the Sierra Nevada.

**5 Palacio de Carlos V**

This Italian Renaissance palace **(left)** is the masterpiece of Pedro Machuca, a student of Michelangelo. Inside are the Museo de Bellas Artes and the Museo de la Alhambra, with its fine collection of Nasrid art.

### 6 Palacios Nazaríes

The Nasrid palaces are built of simple brick, wood and stucco, so as not to compete with the creations of Allah.

**Plan of the Alhambra**

Generalife

### 7 Palacio de Mexuar

The most poorly preserved of the three palaces, this was the most public space, dedicated to judicial and bureaucratic business. The original structure dates from 1365, but in the 16th century the Christians converted it to a chapel.

### 9 Palacio de Comares

Built in the mid-14th century, this area constituted the Serallo, where the sultan would receive dignitaries and deal with diplomatic issues. Inside is the Salón de Embajadores, the main throne room of the Alhambra. In front of the palace is the Patio de Arrayanes **(right)**.

### 10 Palacio de los Leones

Dating from the late 1300s, this palace was the Harem, the private zone reserved for the sultan and his family. The fountain with 12 lions, in the central courtyard of the palace, may represent the 12 signs of the zodiac, the 12 hours of the clock, or the 12 tribes of Israel.

### 8 Partal

As you leave the Alhambra, stroll through the gardens with their watercourses laid out in an area that used to have palaces of its own. All you can see of them now are five porticoed arches **(above)**. This area leads up to the Generalife *(see pp14–15)*.

**NEED TO KNOW**

**MAP S2**

*The Alhambra:* 958 02 79 71; open Apr–mid-Oct: 8:30am–8pm daily, 10–11:30pm Tue–Sat; mid-Oct–Mar: 8:30am–6pm daily, 8–9:30pm Fri & Sat; closed 1 Jan, 25 Dec; adm €18, €19.09 (online), €10 (night visits); www.tickets.alhambra-patronato.es

*Museo de la Alhambra:* open mid-Mar–mid-Oct: 8:30am–2:30pm Sun & Tue (Wed–Sat: to 8pm); mid-Oct–mid-Mar: 8:30am–2:30pm Sun & Tue (Wed–Sat: to 6pm); closed Mon, 1 Jan, 25 Dec

■ You must carry official ID issued by the government to visit the complex.

■ Visitor numbers are restricted, so book tickets online in advance.

# Moorish Granada: Generalife

**Plan of Generalife**

The Torre de los Picos

## 1 The Towers

Following the gardens of the Partal (see p13) as you walk towards the Generalife, you will encounter a number of restored Moorish towers built into the wall. The Torre de los Picos, Torre del Cadí, Torre de la Cautiva, Torre de las Infantas, Torre del Cabo de la Carrera and Torre del Agua are all worth a look for their fine detail, as well as for the views they command. The Torre de la Cautiva and the Torre de las Infantas are twin tower-palaces with richly decorated rooms.

## 2 Patio de los Cipreses

The Court of the Cypresses is also known as the Patio of the Sultana, for this is where Zoraya, the wife of Boabdil (see p43), is said to have secretly met her lover, the chief of the Abencerrajes clan. The sultan had the chief's men massacred upon discovery of the infidelity. A 700-year-old cypress tree commemorates the trysting place.

## 3 The Hill of the Sun

A footbridge flanked by two towers takes you over to the hill that rises above the Alhambra. A vast summer palace once stood here, amid an enormous garden, which predated the Alhambra by more than a century, although little of it remains today.

## 4 The Name of the Garden

The word Generalife is generally considered to be a corruption of the Arab phrase *Djinat al-Arif*, which can be translated as "the Architect's Garden" (referring to Allah) or simply the "Best" or "High" garden. The Darro River was diverted 18 km (11 miles) to provide water for this lush sanctuary.

Patio de los Cipreses

### HISTORY OF THE ALHAMBRA

The castle was the last bastion of al-Andalus, the Moorish hegemony that, at its height, included almost the entire Iberian Peninsula. By 1237 the Christians had reconquered all but this emirate. The Moors managed to flourish for some 250 years longer, only falling to the forces of King Fernando and Queen Isabel in 1492 *(see p42)*. The Generalife was the summer palace where the Moorish leaders could escape political life and the bustling city below and relax in the landscaped grounds. After centuries of neglect, and attempts by Napoleon's army to blow up the palace, the structures were preserved in the early 19th century, after the American writer Washington Irving inspired the world with his *Tales of the Alhambra (see p55)*.

### ⑤ Teatro

As you climb the hill, you will encounter the amphitheatre, nestled into a tree-lined hollow. Dance performances and musical concerts are offered here as part of an annual festival of the arts.

### ⑥ Jardines Altos

As you reach the entrance to the upper gardens, you will encounter the Patio de Polo, where visitors would leave their horses before ascending to the palace.

**Wisteria in the Jardines Altos**

On this level there is a series of fountains and formal plantings, joined by walkways and copses.

### ⑦ Jardines Nuevos

It is clear the "New Gardens", also called the Lower Gardens, owe little to Moorish taste. Hedges and formal patterns echo Italian style, but the sound of running water creates an atmosphere in keeping with the Moorish ideal. In Islam, Paradise is defined as an oasis – a water garden full of blossoms.

**Patio de la Acequia fountains**

### ⑧ Patio de la Acequia

The "Court of the Long Pool" is the most famous water spectacle of the garden. Perfectly proportioned pools are set off by rows of water jets. At one end stands one of the complex's most harmonious buildings, the Sala Regia, with its decorated arcades and airy portico.

### ⑨ Escalera del Agua

These staircases above the palace, also known as the Camino de las Cascadas, have handrails that double as watercourses. It is best viewed in spring.

### ⑩ Leaving the Gardens

As you exit the gardens you will pass along the Paseo de las Adelfas and the Paseo de los Cipreses, lined respectively with oleanders and cypresses. Back to the Hill of the Sun, stroll down the pretty Cuesta del Rey Chico to the Albaicín *(see pp16–17)*.

# Moorish Granada: Albaicín

**Mudéjar-style Iglesia de Santa Ana**

## ① Iglesia de Santa Ana
MAP R2 ▪ C/Santa Ana 1

At the end of Plaza Nueva stands this 16th-century brick church in Mudéjar style, built by Muslim artisans for Christian patrons. Inside the main chapel is a coffered ceiling in the Moorish tradition. The bell tower was originally a minaret.

## ② Paseo de los Tristes
MAP S2

The broad tree-lined esplanade follows the course of the river upstream. It once accommodated tournaments, processions and funeral cortèges, but now bars and restaurants dominate the scene.

## ③ Casa de Castril
MAP R2 ▪ Carrera del Darro 43 ▪ 600 14 31 41 ▪ Open Jul–Aug: 9am–3pm Tue–Sun; Sep–Jun: 9am–8pm Tue–Sat, 9am–3pm Sun

This ornate 16th-century mansion was originally owned by the secretary to King Fernando and Queen Isabel. Since 1879 it has served as the Archaeological and Ethnological Museum, displaying artifacts from Granada's past, from the Paleolithic era up until the Reconquest in 1492. The remarkable collection is displayed across three galleries and around the central courtyard.

## ④ Iglesia de San Pedro y San Pablo
MAP R2 ▪ Carrera del Darro 2

Across from the Casa de Castril, this church, built in the 1500s, graces an attractive spot on the banks of the river. From here you can see the Alhambra dominating the landscape.

## ⑤ Real Chancillería
MAP Q2 ▪ Plaza del Padre Suárez 1

The austerely impressive Royal Chancery dates from 1530, built shortly after the *reconquista* as part of the futile attempt to Christianize this Moorish quarter. The palace is attributed to architect Diego de Siloé.

**Real Chancillería, now the high court**

## ⑥ El Bañuelo (Baños Árabes)
MAP R2 ▪ Carrera del Darro 31 ▪ 958 57 51 31 ▪ Open daily

Dating from the 11th century, these are the best preserved Moorish baths in Spain. They comprise several rooms that were used for changing, meeting, massage and bathing.

**The old Moorish baths of El Bañuelo**

**El Mirador de San Nicolás, offering fine views of the Alhambra**

### 7 El Mirador de San Nicolás
MAP R1

In front of the Iglesia de San Nicolás, this magnificent terrace has such lovely views of the Alhambra and the Sierra Nevada that it has long been dubbed El Mirador ("The Lookout Point") de San Nicolás. The views are extraordinary at sunset, when the Alhambra glows softly ochre and the often snowcapped Sierra Nevada radiates pink in the distance.

### 8 Plaza Larga
MAP R1

From the Paseo de los Tristes follow Calle Panaderos to reach this busy market square, where you'll mostly find produce stalls as well as cheap restaurants and bars. The square sports an Islamic gateway with a typically angled entrance as part

**Map of Albaicín**

of what remains of the upper fortifications. This is the Arco de las Pesas – if you pass through it you will come to the Albaicín's most popular square, Plaza San Nicolás.

### 9 Tearooms

As you wander around the labyrinth of whitewashed houses and tiny sloping alleyways of the Albaicín quarter you will encounter many tearooms – a Moroccan tradition that is very much alive in this quarter. Possibly the best one, La Tetería del Bañuelo (see p122), consists of a series of rooms set amid delightful gardens. Here you can sip your minty brew, nibble honeyed sweets and contemplate the timeless panorama.

### 10 Moroccan Shops

Check out the hilly streets off Calle Elvira, especially Caldería Vieja and Caldería Nueva, for typically Moroccan shops. The scene is indistinguishable from what you would find in Morocco itself, with the colourful wares spilling out onto the pavements (see p120).

---

**SACROMONTE GYPSY CAVES**

Leaving the Albaicín quarter to the north, follow the Camino del Sacromonte to reach the hill of the same name. The so-called "Holy Hill" is most noted for the presence of some 3,500 caves traditionally inhabited by gypsies (see p50). For more than six centuries, the zone has been known for *zambras* and impromptu gypsy fiestas of flamenco music and dance, and visitors have always been welcome to witness these cultural celebrations. Today some 80 per cent of the caves are still occupied, and several of them continue to operate as venues for flamenco tableaus.

# TOP 10 ⭐ Seville Cathedral and La Giralda

Seville's cathedral is an arresting sight not only for its size but also for its mighty Moorish bell tower, La Giralda. A visit here is a great introduction to Seville's Islamic and Christian heritage. The cathedral occupies the site of a mosque built by the Almohads in the 12th century. In 1248, after some 500 years of Islamic rule, Seville was reconquered by Christian forces, who rededicated the mosque to the Virgin and used it as their principal place of worship. It was demolished in 1401 and it took just over a century to erect the new cathedral, the largest in Europe.

### 1 Exterior and Scale

In sheer cubic vastness, Seville Cathedral **(right)** is the largest Christian church *(see p86)* in the world, and there's a certificate from the Guinness Book of Records on display here to prove it. It measures 126 m (415 ft) by 83 m (270 ft) and the nave rises to 43 m (140 ft). The best place to take it all in is from La Giralda.

### 2 Cathedral Paintings

There are around 600 paintings throughout the cathedral, from the entrance pavilion to the sacristies, together with sculptures from the 17th-century Sevillian School, which included artists Bartolomé Esteban Murillo, Francisco de Zurbarán and Francisco Pacheco.

### 3 Puerta del Perdón

The "Gate of Forgiveness" is set in a crenellated wall and is the main entrance to the one surviving part of the mosque. The arch and bronze doors are a masterpiece of Almohad art, carved with 880 Koranic inscriptions. Sculpted Renaissance elements include a bas-relief of the Expulsion of the Moneychangers from the Temple.

### 4 Sacristía de los Cálices

Part of the cathedral's treasury is housed here. The anteroom displays the Tenebrario, a 7.8-m (25-ft) Plateresque candelabrum used during Holy Week. Inside, the star turns are a painting by Goya of Seville's patron saints, Justa and Rufina, as well as canvases by Zurbarán, Jordaens and other Masters.

### 5 Sacristía Mayor

The Main Sacristy **(left)** is dominated by a dome, designed in the 16th century. The centrepiece of the sacristy is a 450-kg (990-lb), 3-m (10-ft) silver Baroque monstrance created by Juan de Arfe.

### 6 Patio de los Naranjos

The Courtyard of Orange Trees was the place where ritual ablutions were performed before entering the mosque for prayer.

### 7 Interior

The vast Gothic arches that line the nave inside the cathedral are so high that the space within the building is said to have its own independent climate.

### 8 La Giralda

This grand tower (below) is the symbol of Seville, built between 1172 and 1195 (see p86). It takes its name from the weathervane on top, called *El Giraldillo*.

**SEMANA SANTA FESTIVITIES**

Seville's Holy Week celebrations (see p80) are Andalucía's richest. Here, 61 *cofradías* (brotherhoods) compete to bear aloft the most well-dressed Virgin in mourning and an image from the Passion of Christ. Floats are carried by *costaleros* (bearers), while the processions are led by *nazarenos* – penitents in hoods and robes.

**Plan of Seville Cathedral**

### 9 Sala Capitular

The Chapter House contains Murillo's *Immaculate Conception* in the vault and has a lavish marble floor.

### 10 Capilla Mayor

The main altar's *tour de force* is its 15th-century *retablo* – the world's largest altarpiece (below). Composed of gilded carved wood, it features some 45 Biblical scenes employing some 1,000 figures.

**NEED TO KNOW**

**MAP M4** ■ Plaza Virgen de los Reyes ■ 954 21 49 71 ■ www.catedralde sevilla.es

**Open** 11am–7pm Mon–Sat, 2:30–7pm Sun; services: check website for timings

Adm €11 online (€1 increase in price if bought on-site; includes access to La Giralda); audio guides €5 (€4 in app format)

Guided tours and rooftop tours available in English (check website for details)

■ For great views, head to the rooftop bar at EME Catedral Hotel (see p140).

■ It's a rewarding climb up the sloping La Giralda.

# TOP 10 ⭐ Real Alcázar, Seville

This extensive complex embodies a series of palatial rooms and spaces from various ages. The front towers and walls are the oldest surviving section, dating from 913 CE and built by the Emir of Córdoba, Abd ar-Rahman III, most likely on the ruins of Roman barracks. A succession of caliphs added their dazzling architectural statements over the ensuing centuries. Then came the Christian kings, particularly Pedro I in the 14th century, and finally the rather perfunctory 16th-century apartments of Carlos V.

Plan of the Real Alcázar

### 1 Puerta del León

The entrance gate into the first courtyard (above) is flanked by original Almohad walls. Note the Gothic and Arabic inscriptions on the interior façade.

### 2 Sala de Justicia

Here and in adjacent halls and courts is some of the purest Mudéjar art commissioned by Alfonso XI of Castile around 1330 and executed by crafters from Granada. The star-shaped coffered ceiling and fine plasterwork are quite exquisite.

### 3 Patio de las Muñecas

The intimate Courtyard of the Dolls was the private living room of the palace and supposedly gets its name from two faces carved into the base of one of the arches.

### 4 Patio de las Doncellas

The Courtyard of the Maidens (above) commemorates the annual tribute of 100 virgins delivered to the Moorish rulers by the Christians. Look out for the fine *azulejos* (tiles).

### 5 Salón de Embajadores

The most brilliant room in the entire Alcázar, its crowning glory is the dazzling dome of carved, painted and gilded wood (above), constructed by crafters from Toledo and completed in 1366.

### 6 Patio de la Montería

The Hunting Courtyard has 14th-century Mudéjar decorative work – a perfect mix of cultural influences.

### 7 Casa de la Contratación

The halls in the House of Trade are where Fernando and Isabel met with the explorers of the Americas.

**PEDRO I**

Few Spanish kings have received such contradictory press over the centuries as Pedro I (1350–69). Called both "the Cruel" – el Cruel – and "the Avenger" – el Justiciero – he killed his own brother in order to consolidate his position and flaunted his cohabitation with his mistress María de Padilla. The Alcázar we see today is almost entirely the result of Pedro's rebuilding programme, primarily so that he and María would have a cosy place of retreat.

### 8 Patio del Yeso

The secluded Courtyard of Plaster, greatly restored, is one of the few remnants of the 12th-century palace. The delicate stucco work features scalloped arches (right) and is set off by a garden with water channels.

### 9 Palacio Gótico

In a refurbished 13th-century Gothic structure built by Alfonso X the Wise, this palace has a rather inharmonious Renaissance style.

### 10 Gardens

Moorish touches such as fountains, pools, orange groves, palms and hedgerows abound in these gardens (left). Concerts and events are held here on summer evenings.

**NEED TO KNOW**

**MAP M4** ■ Patio de Banderas ■ 954 50 23 24 ■ www.alcazarsevilla.org

**Open** 9:30am–7pm daily (Oct–Mar: to 5pm); closed 1 & 6 Jan, Good Friday, 25 Dec

Adm: €13.50 (€14.50 with online booking fee); €5.50 (for Royal Bedroom); free Mon (Apr–Sep: 6–7pm, Oct–Mar: 4–5pm)

■ A flow-control entry system allows a limited number of people into the Alcázar every half hour. To avoid long waits, visit at off-peak times.

■ There are 30-minute evening tours with re-enactments of the Alcázar's history in Spanish; book tickets in advance.

# TOP 10 ⭐ Córdoba

This city is a jewel in Andalucía's crown. The main sight is undoubtedly the Great Mosque, La Mezquita – one of the unsurpassed masterpieces of world architecture. In addition to the mosque and its incongruous but splendid cathedral within, other sights here include fine monuments and palaces from every age, art and history museums, one of Andalucía's greatest archaeological repositories, and a museum dedicated to the history of the bullfight.

### 4 Palacio de los Marqueses de Viana

A former noble residence (14th- to 18th-century), the museum includes preserved period rooms and furnishings.

### 5 Museo Taurino

Dedicated to bullfighting, this museum is home to a fine collection of art on the theme. Its spectacular exhibits showcase the history of the bullfight, the rearing of the bulls as well as important figures in bullfighting.

### 1 Judería

The city's ancient Jewish quarter **(above)**, dates back to the time of the Roman Empire. Its narrow alleyways, brilliantly whitewashed and hung with flowerpots, are graced with beautiful Moorish patios. This district also has Andalucía's only medieval synagogue.

### 2 Plaza del Potro

This small but elegant square, adorned with a 16th-century fountain, was once Córdoba's livestock market.

### 3 La Mezquita

The world's third-largest mosque *(see pp24–5)* remains a place of immense grandeur and mystical power.

### 5 Salón de Embajadores

The most brilliant room in the entire Alcázar, its crowning glory is the dazzling dome of carved, painted and gilded wood **(above)**, constructed by crafters from Toledo and completed in 1366.

### 6 Patio de la Montería

The Hunting Courtyard has 14th-century Mudéjar decorative work – a perfect mix of cultural influences.

### 7 Casa de la Contratación

The halls in the House of Trade are where Fernando and Isabel met with the explorers of the Americas.

### PEDRO I

Few Spanish kings have received such contradictory press over the centuries as Pedro I (1350–69). Called both "the Cruel" – el Cruel – and "the Avenger" – el Justiciero – he killed his own brother in order to consolidate his position and flaunted his cohabitation with his mistress María de Padilla. The Alcázar we see today is almost entirely the result of Pedro's rebuilding programme, primarily so that he and María would have a cosy place of retreat.

### 8 Patio del Yeso

The secluded Courtyard of Plaster, greatly restored, is one of the few remnants of the 12th-century palace. The delicate stucco work features scalloped arches **(right)** and is set off by a garden with water channels.

### 9 Palacio Gótico

In a refurbished 13th-century Gothic structure built by Alfonso X the Wise, this palace has a rather inharmonious Renaissance style.

### 10 Gardens

Moorish touches such as fountains, pools, orange groves, palms and hedgerows abound in these gardens **(left)**. Concerts and events are held here on summer evenings.

---

**NEED TO KNOW**

**MAP M4** ■ Patio de Banderas ■ 954 50 23 24 ■ www.alcazarsevilla.org

**Open** 9:30am–7pm daily (Oct–Mar: to 5pm); closed 1 & 6 Jan, Good Friday, 25 Dec

Adm: €13.50 (€14.50 with online booking fee); €5.50 (for Royal Bedroom); free Mon (Apr–Sep: 6–7pm, Oct–Mar: 4–5pm)

■ A flow-control entry system allows a limited number of people into

the Alcázar every half hour. To avoid long waits, visit at off-peak times.

■ There are 30-minute evening tours with re-enactments of the Alcázar's history in Spanish; book tickets in advance.

# TOP 10 ★ Córdoba

This city is a jewel in Andalucía's crown. The main sight is undoubtedly the Great Mosque, La Mezquita – one of the unsurpassed masterpieces of world architecture. In addition to the mosque and its incongruous but splendid cathedral within, other sights here include fine monuments and palaces from every age, art and history museums, one of Andalucía's greatest archaeological repositories, and a museum dedicated to the history of the bullfight.

### 4 Palacio de los Marqueses de Viana

A former noble residence (14th- to 18th-century), the museum includes preserved period rooms and furnishings.

### 5 Museo Taurino

Dedicated to bullfighting, this museum is home to a fine collection of art on the theme. Its spectacular exhibits showcase the history of the bullfight, the rearing of the bulls as well as important figures in bullfighting.

### 1 Judería

The city's ancient Jewish quarter **(above)**, dates back to the time of the Roman Empire. Its narrow alleyways, brilliantly whitewashed and hung with flowerpots, are graced with beautiful Moorish patios. This district also has Andalucía's only medieval synagogue.

### 2 Plaza del Potro

This small but elegant square, adorned with a 16th-century fountain, was once Córdoba's livestock market.

### 3 La Mezquita

The world's third-largest mosque (see pp24–5) remains a place of immense grandeur and mystical power.

**NEED TO KNOW**

**MAP D3**

*Alcázar and Baños:* Campo Santo de los Mártires; 957 42 01 51; open summer: 8:15am–2:45pm Tue–Sun & hols; winter: 8:15am–8pm Tue–Fri, 9:30am–6pm Sat, 8:15am–2:45pm Sun & hols; adm Alcázar €5, Baños €3

*Palacio de los Marqueses de Viana:* Plaza Don Gome 2; 957 49 67 41; open summer: 9am–3pm Tue–Sun; winter: 10am–7pm Tue–Sat (Sun: to 3pm); adm €10

*Museo Taurino:* Plaza de Maimónides; 957 20 10 56; open 8:45am–

3:15pm Tue–Sun & hols; closed Mon; adm €4; www. museotaurinodecordoba.es

*Museo Torre de la Calahorra:* Puente Romano; 957 29 39 29; open May–Sep: 8:15am–2:45pm daily; Oct–Apr: 8:15am–8pm Tue–Fri, 9:30am–6pm Sat, 8:15am–2:45pm Sun & hols; adm €4.50

*Museo Arqueológico:* Plaza Jerónimo Páez 7; 957 35 55 17; open hours same as Museo de Bellas Artes; adm €1.50

*Museo de Bellas Artes:* Plaza del Potro 1; 957 10 36 59; open summer: 9am–3pm Tue–Sun; winter: 9am–9pm Tue–Sat (Sun: to 3pm); adm €1.50

**Map of Córdoba**

### 7 Museo Arqueológico

Housed in a Renaissance mansion is this excellent archaeological museum. One highlight is the 10th-century Moorish bronze of a stag, which was found at Medina Azahara (see p125).

---

**MULTICULTURAL TRADITION**

Córdoba's brilliance owes much to its rich multicultural history. Its most important edifices are emblematic of the amalgamation of Islamic, Christian and Jewish cultures. In the 10th century, Córdoba was the spiritual and scientific centre of the Western World, due to its policy of religious tolerance (see p42). After the *reconquista*, many non-Christian thinkers were banished and the city fell into decline.

---

### 8 Puente Romano

Crossing Río Guadalquivir, this bridge (left), has Roman foundations. A statue in the middle honours Archangel Raphael, said to have saved the city from the plague.

### 9 Museo de Bellas Artes

A former 16th-century charity hospital is now the city's main art museum. It has a collection of works by local painters and sculptors, as well as paintings and drawings by masters such as Goya, Ribera, Murillo Valdés Leal and Zurbarán.

### 6 Museo Torre de la Calahorra

Part of a Moorish castle that controlled access to the city, the tower now houses the Roger Garaudy Three Cultures Museum, which explains how all religions lived side by side in medieval Córdoba and houses exhibits from the time (right). There are great views of the city from the tower.

### 10 Alcázar de los Reyes Cristianos

This fortified palace, built in 1328, was used by the Inquisition (1500s–1820) and as a prison (until the 1950s). Today it is tranquil, with gardens, water terraces and fountains (left). Also visit the Baños del Alcázar Califal, the Arab baths, which are adjacent.

# TOP 10 ★ La Mezquita, Córdoba

Córdoba's Great Mosque, dating back 12 centuries, is one of the world's finest examples of Islamic architecture. The striking mosque-cathedral, with its rows of hallowed arches, has evolved over the centuries blending many architectural forms. The original mosque was built by Abd el-Rahman I, the founder of the caliphate of Córdoba, on the site of a Visigothic church. Later, during the 16th century a cathedral was built in the heart of the reconsecrated mosque, under the orders of Carlos I, to complete the city's "Christianization".

### 1 The Caliphal Style

The mosque was begun by Caliph Abd el-Rahman I in 786 CE. La Mezquita constitutes the beginning of the Caliphal architectural style, combining Roman, Gothic, Byzantine, Syrian and Persian elements.

### 2 Puerta del Perdón

Originally the mosque had many entrances, designed to let in light. The Gate of Forgiveness (1377) is now the only one open to all (above).

### 3 Torre del Alminar

A minaret once stood where the belfry now is (right). Built in 957, it was enveloped in this Baroque bell tower.

### 4 Interior

The plan of the interior (above) is that of a so-called "forest" mosque, with the rows and rows of variegated columns (856 remaining) and arches designed to resemble palm trees. Unlike Christian churches, based on earlier Roman basilicas with their focus on the central enthroned "judge", the Islamic aim is to induce a meditative state for prayer.

## 5 Patio de los Naranjos

The delightful Courtyard of the Orange Trees would have been used by worshippers to perform ritual ablutions before they went to prayer.

## 6 Recycled Columns

Great ingenuity was required to achieve the rhythmic uniformity inside, since most of the columns used in construction were recycled from Roman, Visigothic and other sources. They were a hotchpotch of varying sizes, so the longer ones had to be sunk into the floor. To reach the desired height, a second tier was then added.

## 7 Capilla de Villaviciosa and Capilla Real

One of the more grand Christian additions, the Villaviciosa Chapel **(above)**, built in 1377, has exuberant Mudéjar arches. Next to it, the Royal Chapel has stucco work and *azulejos* (tiles).

### A SPIRITUAL SITE

This magnificent edifice was not the first religious structure to be built on this spot. The Caliph bought the land from the Christians, who had built the Visigothic Cathedral of St Vincent here. In its last years, that building had been divided by a partition, so that it could serve the needs of both Christian and Muslim communities. The Visigothic structure, in its turn, had been constructed on top of a Roman temple, and its columns are still visible in La Mezquita.

## 8 Mihrab

Dating from the 10th century, this is the jewel of the mosque. An octagonal chamber set into the wall, it was to be the sacred focal point of prayer, directed towards Mecca. No amount of ornamentation was spared. Emperor Nicephorus III sent artisans from Constantinople to create some of the finest Byzantine mosaics in existence **(right)**.

### NEED TO KNOW

**MAP D3** ■ C/del Cardenal Herrero 1, Córdoba ■ 957 47 05 12 ■ www.mezquita-catedraldecordoba.org

**Open** Mar–Oct: 10am–7pm Mon–Sat, 8:30–11:30am & 3–7pm Sun & hols; Nov–Feb: 8:30am–6pm Mon–Sat, 8:30–11:30am & 3–6pm Sun & hols

Adm adults €13; children aged 10–14 €7; under 10s free; 8:30–9:30am Mon–Sat free entry (no groups)

................................................................
■ Last admission is 30 minutes before closing, but try to allow at least an hour to do the site justice.

■ El Caballo Rojo (*C/Cardenal Herrero 28; 957 47 53 75*), located across from the Puerta del Perdón, is a local favourite serving dishes inspired by the Moors. The terrace offers views of the mosque.

## 9 Cathedral

In 1523, some 60 of the 1,013 columns were removed from the mosque to make way for the cathedral.

## 10 Choir Stalls

The Baroque choir stalls date from 1758, and the exquisite carved mahogany depicts Biblical scenes.

**Plan of La Mezquita**

# TOP 10 ⭐ Cádiz

**Map of Cádiz**

The gorgeous city of Cádiz inspired the poet Lord Byron to praise its heavenly blue setting. Nowadays it is one of Andalucía's under-visited treasures. According to ancient chronicles, the city was founded by the Phoenicians as Gadir ("Fortress") in 1104 BCE, giving it a good claim to being Europe's oldest. Under the Romans it became Gades and was notable as the city where Julius Caesar held his first public office.

### 3 Barrio del Pópulo

The Barrio del Pópulo is the medieval heart of the city, which still retains its three 13th-century gates. The main entrance of the surviving 18th-century city wall, the Puerta de Tierra **(left)**, marks the boundary between the old city and the modern part of Cádiz.

### 5 Torre Tavira

The camera obscura in this tower, the city's highest at 46 m (150 ft), offers great views **(above)**.

### 6 Oratorio de la Santa Cueva

This Neo-Classical chapel has an upper church with Ionic columns. Three frescoes by Goya depict miraculous moments from the life of Christ.

### 1 Iglesia de Santa Cruz and Teatro Romano

In the midst of the Barrio del Pópulo are ruins of a Roman theatre and church dating from 1260.

### 2 Hospital de Mujeres

This Baroque former hospital's main attraction is El Greco's *Extasis de San Francisco*.

### 4 Plaza de las Flores

Also known as the Plaza de Topete, this square **(right)** was the sight of a Phoenician temple.

**7 Catedral Nueva**

The "New Cathedral" **(above)** was begun in 1722. The bell tower, or Torre de Poniente (western tower), offers superb views of the city below.

**8 Museo de Cádiz**

Archaeological finds and Baroque paintings are the museum's forte. Exhibits include Roman shipwreck finds and a pair of 5th-century BCE Phoenician sarcophagi, showing Greek and Egyptian influences.

**10 Museo de las Cortes de Cádiz**

A mural in this museum eulogizes Cádiz as the birthplace of liberalism. On 29 March 1812, Spain's first liberal constitution was drawn up here; it played a huge role in shaping modern European politics.

**9 Plaza San Juan de Dios**

On the edge of the Barrio del Pópulo is this 16th-century, palm-fringed plaza **(below)**. Facing the port, it forms the hub of city life (see p58).

**LOS CARNAVALES**

The vibrant Carnaval celebrations in this port town are the most exhilarating in all of Spain (see p80). In fact, so dear is this annual blow-out to *gaditanos* (as the locals call themselves) that it was the only such event in the country that Franco's forces failed to suppress during the decades of dictatorship. The festival's various traditions date back to the 15th century, when the town had a Genoese enclave, though some claim there is also a strong Cuban influence.

**NEED TO KNOW**

**MAP B5**

*Catedral Nueva & Torre de Poniente:* 956 28 61 54; open 10am–8pm Tue–Sat, 1:30–8pm Sun; adm €7 (includes the cathedral and the tower)

*Torre Tavira:* C/Marqués del Real Tesoro 10; 956 21 29 10; open 10am–6pm daily (May–Sep: to 8pm); adm €7

*Hospital de Mujeres:* C/Hospital de Mujeres 26; 956 80 70 18; open 10:30am–4pm Mon–Fri; adm €5

*Museo de Cádiz:* Plaza de Mina; 856 10 50 23; open 9am–9pm Tue–Sat, 9am–3pm Sun & hols; adm €1.50 (free for EU members)

■ Book hotels up to a year ahead for Carnaval.

# TOP 10 ★ Ronda

This is the most famous of the *pueblos blancos* – a scattering of evocative hamlets that reveal their Moorish roots between Málaga, Algeciras and Seville. Ronda is the only town in the wildly mountainous region of the Serranía de Ronda. Located just half an hour's drive from the Costa del Sol, Ronda has managed to retain its timelessness and charm, no matter how busy it gets. Its natural setting is so spectacular that the views alone make it a must-see experience.

### El Tajo and Puente Nuevo ①

Ronda perches upon a sheer outcrop that is split by a precipitous cleft, El Tajo, 100 m (330 ft) deep **(right)**. The spectacular 18th-century Puente Nuevo bridge links the old city, La Ciudad, with the new.

### ② Casa del Rey Moro

A visit to the gardens of this 18th-century mansion, built on the foundations of a Moorish palace, will provide superb views.

### ④ Palacio del Marqués de Salvatierra

The carved stone portal outside this 18th-century mansion features four figures that are believed to represent the Indigenous Peoples of South America.

### ③ Baños Árabes

These wonderfully preserved Moorish baths **(above)** date from the 1200s or early 1300s. The multiple barrel vaulting pierced with star-shaped lunettes is typical of such structures, but the octagonal brick columns supporting horseshoe arches are highly original.

**NEED TO KNOW**

**MAP D5**

*Casa del Rey Moro:* C/Cuesta de Santo Domingo 9; open May–Sep: 10am–9:30pm daily (Oct–Apr: to 8pm daily); adm €7; www. casadelreymoro.org

*Baños Árabes:* Barrio de Padre Jesús; 656 95 09 37; open 9:30am–8pm Tue–Fri, 10am–2pm & 3–8pm Sat & Mon (Sun: to 3pm); adm €4.50

*Palacio de Mondragón:* 952 87 08 18; opening hours same as Baños Árabes; adm €4

*Plaza de Toros:* C/Virgen de la Paz 15; adm €9; open 10am–6pm daily (Mar–Oct: to 7pm); www.rmcr.org

*Museo Lara Coleccionismo:* C/Armiñán 29; open Jun–Oct: 11am–8pm daily (Nov–May: to 7pm daily; adm €4; www.museolara.org

*Iglesia de Santa María la Mayor:* Plaza Duquesa de Parcent; 952 87 40 48; open 10am–8pm Mon–Sat, 10am–12:30pm & 2–8pm Sun; adm €4.50

*Previous pages* Cycling by the scenic waterfront in Cádiz

### 6 Palacio de Mondragón

One of Ronda's most beautiful palaces dates from 1314. Some of the original mosaic work, a magnificent Mudéjar ceiling and shady inner courtyards **(left)** can still be seen. Part of the palace is now the city's archaeological museum.

**THE ORIGINS OF BULLFIGHTING**

The creation here of the Real Maestranza de Caballería (Royal Academy of Knights) in 1572 set the stage for the birth of bullfighting. The Maestranza trained Spain's aristocracy to ride and students on horseback would challenge wild bulls. Legend tells that when one rider fell from his horse and was attacked by a bull, a bystander distracted the animal by waving his hat. The man's grandson, Pedro Romero (1749–1839), perfected the art.

#### Map of Ronda

### 5 Puente Viejo and Puente de San Miguel

The Puente Viejo (Old Bridge) dates from 1616 and may be a rebuilding of a Roman span across the gorge, though it is believed by some that its pedigree is Moorish, like the Puente de San Miguel.

### 7 Minarete de San Sebastián

This 14th-century tower is all that remains of a Nasrid mosque and the church of San Sebastián that was built on top of it.

### 8 Plaza de Toros

Inaugurated in 1785, Ronda's bullring **(left)** was constructed in limestone in an elegant double-tiered sweep; it is the widest in the world and one of the oldest in Spain. Ronda is the birthplace and spiritual home of Spanish bullfighting, and houses a museum – the Museo Taurino – dedicated to the tradition.

### 9 Museo Lara Coleccionismo

With over 2,000 works, this museum holds the largest private collection in Spain. Objects include cultural artifacts, antique clocks, weapons and scientific instruments.

### 10 Iglesia de Santa María la Mayor

Much of this church includes a 13th-century mosque, notably the base of the Mudéjar belfry.

# 🔟 ⭐ The Costa del Sol

The former fishing villages of the "Sun Coast" welcome millions of international visitors each year – not counting the estimated 300,000 expats who call the coast home. The winning formula is 320 sunny days a year, warm waters and beaches, a good selection of museums, and good-value entertainment options. Heavy on neon and tower blocks, most of what's here has little to do with local culture, but what is exuberantly Andalucían is the verve with which visitors enjoy themselves in the sun – and party well into the night.

**① Estepona**
The first major resort on this coast is an excellent quieter choice, with 19 km (12 miles) of beach. In the *casco antiguo* (old town), Plaza Las Flores retains considerable charm.

**Marbella ②**
The 15th-century Plaza de los Naranjos is the heart of old town Marbella *(see p65)*, Spain's most expensive resort. Nearby Puerto Banús is the town's glittering marina **(right)**, where you can admire the fabulous yachts and glimpse luxurious lifestyles.

**⑤ Mijas**
Visit this beautiful little village nestled in the mountains **(left)** for views of the coast, as well as the maze of old Moorish streets filled with delightful shops in its tiny squares.

**③ Fuengirola**
This large resort is the most family-orientated, with a good beach and a seafront promenade. There is a restored 10th-century Moorish castle.

**Benalmádena ④**
This resort comes in three parts: the old town inland; the beach and port area **(right)**; and Arroyo de la Miel, a lively suburb.

### 6 Torremolinos

Torre de los Molinos (Tower of the Windmills) refers to a Moorish watchtower that was once surrounded by 19 flourmills. The ancient Torre Vigia is still here, but today it is a hotspot for family vacations. It also has the largest LGBTQ+ scene in the region.

### 7 Málaga

Andalucía's second largest city **(above)** has outposts of Paris's Pompidou Centre and the State Russian Museum – part of a "mile of art". The redeveloped port has given Málaga *(see p104)* dozens of dining options while the nearby Soho district brings art to the streets.

### 8 Torre del Mar

Favoured by Spanish families, this resort is less tawdry than others to the west. It has a wide sandy beach backed by a tree-lined promenade *(see p65)*.

**FRANCO'S DREAM**

It was General Franco, Spain's dictator until 1975, who had the idea of transforming the impoverished fishing villages into the "Florida of Europe". He enacted his plan in the 1960s with money loaned by the US, in return for the right to build nuclear bases on Spanish soil. The jet-set glamour and cheap package deals were a runaway success and by the 1970s the area was an aesthetic and environmental disaster. Since the 1980s, steps have been taken to clean it up.

### 9 Vélez-Málaga

This market town has beautiful Mudéjar features and a lively annual flamenco guitar competition every July.

### 10 Nerja

The whitewashed town of Nerja **(above)** sits on attractive, verdant cliffs with quiet pebble beach coves below *(see p65)*.

**Map of the Costa del Sol**

Estepona · Puerto Banús · Marbella · Mijas · Fuengirola · Benalmádena · Torremolinos · Málaga · Vélez-Málaga · Torrox · Torre del Mar · Nerja

**NEED TO KNOW**

**MAP D5–E5**

*Estepona:* Tourist office, Plaza de las Flores; 952 80 20 02

*Marbella:* Tourist office, Glorieta de la Fontanilla; 952 76 87 60

*Fuengirola:* Tourist office, Plaza Theresa Zabell 32; 952 46 74 57

*Benalmádena:* Tourist office, Avda Antonio Machado 10; 952 44 24 94

*Mijas:* Tourist office, Plaza Virgen de la Peña 2; 952 58 90 34

*Torremolinos:* Tourist office, Paseo Marítimo de La Carihuela; 608 20 88 71

*Málaga:* Tourist office, Plaza de la Marina 11; 951 92 60 20

*Nerja:* Tourist office, C/Carmen 1; 952 52 15 31

# TOP 10 ★ Baeza and Úbeda

These two Jaén Province towns, only 9 km (5.5 miles) apart, are like matching jewel boxes overflowing with Renaissance architectural treasure, and so were awarded the title of UNESCO World Heritage Sites in 2003. Of the two, quiet Baeza has managed to stay almost completely out of the modern age, while Úbeda is now a thriving town with many seasonal attractions. Nevertheless, its stunning historic district is, if anything, the more spectacular.

### **1** Plaza del Pópulo, Baeza

The town's most charming area, the Plaza del Pópulo, is in the midst of Renaissance edifices. It is also called the Square of the Lions, after its fountain, which has four stone lions and a female figure **(right)**.

### **2** Puerta de Jaén, Baeza

A section of the ancient wall, the Jaén Gate, supports an additional arch with coats-of-arms set above.

### **3** Plaza Santa María and Catedral, Baeza

Several glorious 16th-century structures, including the cathedral, front this square. One of the many masterpieces by Renaissance architect Andrés de Vandelvira, the cathedral was originally a Gothic church, built over a mosque in the 13th century.

### **4** Paseo de la Constitución, Baeza

The 16th-century Alhóndiga (Corn Exchange) has elegant three-tiered arches, while the Torre de los Aliatares is a remnant of the old wall *(see p59)*.

### **5** Palacio de Jabalquinto, Baeza

One of the most unusually decorated palaces, the 15th-century Palacio de Jabalquinto **(left)** is sprinkled with coats of arms and stone studs in Isabelline Plateresque style *(see p47)*.

### 6 Plaza San Lorenzo, Úbeda

The Casa de las Torres features two vast square towers with gargoyles, while the Church of San Lorenzo rests on the parapet of the old wall.

### 7 Plaza de San Pedro, Úbeda

Visit the patio of the Real Monasterio de Santa Clara, the town's oldest church **(right)**, where the nuns will sell you their distinctly Arabic *dulces* (sweetcakes). The Palacio de la Rambla is another Vandelvira creation, now home to a luxury hotel *(see p145)*.

**ARCHITECTURE OF THE SPANISH RENAISSANCE**

Spanish Renaissance architecture divides into three periods: Plateresque, Classical High Renaissance and Herrerean. The first refers to the carved detailing on silverwork (*platero* means silversmith), a carry-over from the late Gothic style popular under Queen Isabel. The High Renaissance style is noted for its symmetry and its Greco-Roman imagery. Herrerean works are very sober, practically devoid of decoration.

### 10 Plaza de Vázquez de Molina, Úbeda

Notable on this square is the Capilla del Salvador **(below)**. The Plateresque main front marks a high point in the Spanish Renaissance *(see p45)*.

### 8 The Pottery Quarter, Úbeda

Passing through the Puerta del Losal, a splendid 13th-century Mudéjar gate, takes you into the town's age-old pottery quarter *(see p128)*. Here, modern ceramic artists renowned all over Spain and beyond ply their ancient trade **(above)**.

### 9 Plaza del Primero de Mayo, Úbeda

The variety of riches here includes the Iglesia de San Pablo, displaying an array of styles, the 15th-century Casa Mudéjar – now an archaeological museum – and the 16th-century Ayuntamiento Viejo, with its superb arcades.

---

**NEED TO KNOW**

**MAP F2**

*Baeza:* Tourist office, Casa del Pópulo, Plaza del Pópulo; 953 77 99 82; open 9am–7:30pm Mon–Fri, 9:30am–3pm Sat, Sun & hols; www.ubedaybaezaturismo.com.

*Úbeda:* Tourist office, Plaza Andalucía 5; 953 75 01 38; open 9am–7:30pm Mon–Fri, 9:30am–3pm & 5–7:30pm Sat, Sun & hols; www.turismodeubeda.com

■ In Úbeda, have a drink in the courtyard of the Parador Condestable Dávalos, a 16th-century palace located at the town centre *(see p142)*.

■ Baeza's Restaurante Juanito (*Avda del Alcalde Puché Pardo 57, 953 74 00 40*) is a good place to try regional food.

■ The Úbeda potters are all located along Calle Valencia; look for the workshops of the premier ceramists, the Tito family.

# TOP 10 ⭐ Parque Nacional de Doñana

Established in 1969, the Parque Nacional de Doñana is an important wetland reserve and a prime site for migrating birds. It covers more than 2,470 sq km (954 sq miles) and its wide variety of ecosystems, rare fauna and abundance of bird life are so vital to the overall environmental stability of Western Europe that it is designated a UNESCO Biosphere Reserve. It yields up its natural wonders gradually, but a trip to western Andalucía is not complete without a visit here.

### 1 Setting and History
Located at the estuary of the Guadalquivir River, the area probably owes its present pristine condition to the fact that it was set aside as a hunting preserve for the nobility in the 16th century.

### 4 Habitats
The park features three distinct kinds of ecosystem: dunes **(left)**, *coto* (pine and cork forests and scrubland) and *marisma* (wetlands), which in turn comprise marshes, salt marshes, lagoons and floodplains.

**White storks fly over Doñana's wetlands**

### 2 Guided Tours
All-terrain vehicles depart from the Visitor Centres twice daily with itineraries dependent on the time of year. The marshes dry up during the summer months, limiting birdwatching, but this increases the chance of seeing rare mammals.

### 5 Fauna
The endangered pardel lynx **(right)** is the emblem of the park. At least 300,000 birds make their home here, including the flamingo and the purple gallinule. Around 25 pairs of the very rare Iberian eagle also survive here.

### 3 El Rocío's Romería
This town **(below)** is the focal point of one of Spain's largest festivals, the Romería del Rocío *(see p80)*. The four-day pilgrimage leading up to Whitsun winds its way through the park. Thousands honour the Virgin of El Rocío.

### 6 Visitor Centres
Visitor Centres, such as Centro de Información La Rocina, offer exhibitions as well as planned trails, with rest areas and birdwatching options.

### Flora 7

Umbrella pines and cork-oaks flourish here and both types of tree provide crucial nesting sites for birds. Wild flowers in the dunes and scrubland areas include the bright pink spiny-leafed thrift **(right)**, besom heath, yellow gorse and the bubil lily.

**ECOLOGICAL ISSUES**

Despite efforts to protect the park, in 1998 a Río Tinto mining toxic waste storage reservoir burst, dumping pollutants into the Guadiamar River, one of the wetlands' main tributaries. Thankfully, the wave of acids and heavy metals was stopped just short of the park, but damage was done to its border areas. Today, the park's eco-system is increasingly under threat due to lack of rainfall and illegal water irrigation.

### Bird Shelter 10

The Centro de Visitantes El Acebuche, the main visitor centre, is set on a lagoon. At the eastern end there is an aviary where rescued birds receive intensive care. It's an opportunity for visitors to view some unusual species.

### El Palacio de Acebrón 8

This Neo-Classical style hunting lodge, built in 1961, has an exhibition on the history and ethnography of the region, and offers good views above. It is a starting point for a 12-km (8-mile) woodland trail nearby.

### Huts 9

Dating from the 18th century, these traditional huts **(right)** are found in the *pinares* (pine forests). Sometimes clustered into small villages, the uninhabited structures are made of pine frames covered with local thatch.

**NEED TO KNOW**

**MAP B4** ■ For 4x4 guided tours 959 44 24 74

*Doñana Reservas:* 959 44 24 74; www.donanareservas.com; open two tours daily, hours vary; tours adults €30, under-10s €15

*El Rocío Turismo:* C/Muñoz Pavón; 959 02 66 02

*Centro de Visitantes El Acebuche:* Ctra A483, 3 km (1.5 miles) from Matalascañas; 959 43 96 29

*Centro de Información La Rocina:* Ctra A483, 27 km (17 miles) from El Rocío; 959 43 95 69; open 9am–3pm & 4–6pm daily (Feb–Oct: to 7pm;

mid-Jun–mid-Sep: to 3pm Sun)

■ Bring binoculars, mosquito repellent, sunscreen and walking shoes; watch out for quicksand.

■ If you join in the Romería del Rocío, you will need a sleeping bag and food.

# 🔟 ⭐ The Sierra Nevada

The Sierra Nevada ("Snowy Mountains") include Spain's tallest peaks and are Europe's second-highest mountain range after the Alps. Until the 20th century, their only regular visitors were the so-called *neveros* (icemen), who brought back blocks of ice to sell in nearby Granada, and for years the only part the mountains played in a tour of the region was as the glistening backdrop to the Alhambra. They have now become popular in their own right – for trekking, skiing and exploring the remarkable collection of villages on their southern slopes, Las Alpujarras. The area was made a national park in 1999.

## 1 Setting

Spain's highest peak, the Mulhacén (3,482 m/11,425 ft), is at the western end of the range **(right)**. To the south are fertile valleys.

## 2 Flora and Fauna

Snowcapped most of the year, these heights are still rich in wildflowers. Some 60 varieties are unique here, such as a giant honeysuckle. Fauna include the ibex and the golden eagle.

## 3 Puerto del Suspiro del Moro

Heading south from Granada on the N323, you'll come to the spot known as the "Pass of the Moor's Sigh". Here, the bereft Boabdil (the last Moorish ruler in Spain), expelled by the Christians, is said to have looked back on his beloved city for the last time.

## 4 Barranco de Poqueira

This vast and gorgeous ravine is home to a stunning collection of tiny villages. Much loved by visitors seeking tranquillity, the remote site even has its own Tibetan monastery, founded in 1982. The ravine is an excellent place for easy day walks, and each town offers traditional local crafts.

## 5 Las Alpujarras

The southern side of the Sierra Nevada is a dramatic zone, home to a stunning series of white villages **(left)**. The architecture here is pure Moorish, almost identical to that found in the Rif Mountains of Morocco. Houses are flat-roofed, clustered together and joined by little bridges.

### 8 Skiing

The main ski resort, Sol y Nieve (which means "sun and snow"), is Europe's most southerly, and in operation from December to April or even May. The pistes and facilities **(left)** are good enough to have hosted the world Alpine skiing championships.

### 9 Valle de Lecrín

This bucolic valley is filled with almond, olive and citrus groves – the almond blossom is stunning in late winter.

### 10 Hiking

There is a paved road over the top of the range but the uppermost reaches have been closed to cars since the national park was established in January 1999. In summer it's a hiker's paradise **(right)** – the second-highest peak, Veleta (3,470 m/11,385 ft), is a relatively easy 5-hour round trip.

**BRENAN'S SOUTH FROM GRANADA**

In the 1920s, British writer Gerald Brenan, a member of the Bloomsbury set, came to live in the village of Yegen in the eastern Alpujarras. A plaque in the town marks the house he lived in. He noted his experiences in his book *South from Granada*, a wonderful evocation of the place and its people, whose way of life is still largely unchanged. The 2002 Spanish film *Al Sur de Granada*, based on the book, is a delightful dramatization.

### 6 Órgiva

Made the regional capital in 1839, this town remains the area's largest. It's at its best on Thursday mornings, when everyone comes alive for market day, and you can find traditional local products **(above)**.

### 7 Lanjarón

Famous since Roman times for its mineral springs, the town is now a modern *balneario* (spa) and marks the beginning of the Alpujarras proper. Below the main street is a Moorish castle with great views over the gorge.

**NEED TO KNOW**

**MAP F4** ■ Parque Nacional de la Sierra Nevada, Ctra A 395 – dirección Pradollano – km 23, 18196 Güéjar Sierra ■ 958 98 02 46

*Sierra Nevada Club* (skiing): Plaza de Andalucía 4, Monachil; 902 70 80 90; www.sierranevada.es

■ Lovers of *jamón serrano* (mountain ham) must try the delicious snow-cured version from the town of Trevélez.

■ Extra sun protection is vital here. Hikers and trekkers should have good walking shoes, something to wear against the wind and binoculars.

■ Petrol stations are a rarity in Las Alpujarras. Coming from the west, Órgiva is a good place to fill up.

■ Enjoy Sierra Nevada views from Torre de la Vela in the Alhambra (see pp12–13).

# The Top 10
# of Everything

**Patio de las Doncellas (Courtyard of the Maidens), Real Alcázar, Seville**

# 🔟 Moments in History

## 1 Bronze Age Developments

The Iberian (Tartessian) civilization got its strongest start when bronze began to be smelted and worked in Andalucía around 2500 BCE. Some early tribes built the oldest megalithic tombs (dolmens) in western Europe.

## 2 Phoenician and Greek colonies

Attracted by the area's mineral wealth, the Phoenicians founded a trading post in around 1100 BCE at what is now Cádiz, while the Greeks established a toehold near Málaga in 636 BCE. The two maintained a mercantile rivalry until Carthage, a former Phoenician colony, dominated the region.

## 3 Roman Spain

The first Roman town in Spain, Itálica (see p97), was established in 206 BCE; Rome finally wrested the entire region from the Carthaginians in 201 BCE. Due to abundant local produce, Andalucía became one of the empire's wealthiest outposts.

## 4 Arab Domination

Some 700 years later, when the Roman Empire began to come apart, tribes from northern Europe laid claim to the peninsula. The Vandals and then the Visigoths ruled for some three centuries. Political instability and conflict over rightful succession in 710 CE led to the enlistment of Muslim armies from North Africa. The Moors saw their chance and within 10 years they had taken over.

## 5 Moorish Sophistication

The Moors were custodians of the best features of Roman civilization: religious tolerance, scientific and philosophical thought, engineering and art (see pp48–9). In the 10th century, Córdoba became the largest and wealthiest city in Europe under the Caliphate of Abd ar-Rahman III.

**Moorish La Mezquita, Córdoba**

## 6 Reconquista

The dissolution of the Caliphate in 1031 marked the beginning of the end for Moorish Spain. Some 30 taifas (principalities), jostling for political hegemony, proved no contest for the Christians. The eight-month siege and reconquista of Granada in 1492 was the most poignant loss.

**Itálica's Roman amphitheatre**

**Troops at the Spanish-American War**

### 7 Imperial Collapse

Colonial losses that began in 1713 following the War of Spanish Succession reached their *dénouement* with Spain's defeat in the Spanish-American War of 1898. In Andalucía this long decline meant grinding poverty and mass emigration.

### 8 Franco and the Civil War

The Spanish Civil War (1936–9) was ignited by a military coup led by General Francisco Franco. On 18 July 1936 the war began when Nationalists took Cádiz, Seville and Granada. Then followed the grim years (1939–75) of Franco's dictatorship.

### 9 Seville Expo '92

The World Fair in 1992 celebrated the quincentenary of Columbus's seafaring expedition to the Americas. It brought 42.5 million visitors and a sprucing up of Seville, but left bankruptcy in its wake. After more than a decade of difficulties, numerous efforts to improve the city have resulted in a boom in tourism once again.

### 10 Present-day Andalucía

Andalucía, the most populated region in Spain, faces increasing ecological challenges as the climate crisis escalates. These growing concerns became a hot topic during the 2022 regional elections, where Spain's People's party, a traditional centre-right party, won an absolute majority – the first time to happen in Spanish democracy.

## TOP 10 HISTORIC ANDALUCÍAN FIGURES

**1 Melkarth**
The Phoenician's name for Hercules, whom legend claims to have founded Andalucía.

**2 Trajan**
One of the greatest Roman emperors (98–117 CE) was a native of Itálica.

**3 Hadrian**
Emperor Trajan's successor (117–38 CE) was a great builder, emphasizing Rome's Classical Greek roots.

**4 Abd ar-Rahman III**
The Syrian Emir (912–61 CE) established al-Andalus, an autonomous caliphate.

**5 Isabel and Fernando**
Isabel of Castilla and Fernando of Aragón (1479–1516) were dubbed "The Catholic Monarchs".

**6 Boabdil**
The final Moorish ruler (r.1482–92) lost Granada to the Catholic Monarchs.

**7 Emperor Carlos V**
His reign (1516–56) left Spain nearly bankrupt, but with cultural legacies such as his palace in Granada *(see p12)*.

**8 Felipe V**
Felipe V (1700–46) had his court in Seville until a claim to the throne by Archduke Charles of Austria led to the War of Spanish Succession.

**9 Felipe González**
A native of Seville, this left-wing leader (1982–96) brought rapid change to Spain and to Andalucía.

**10 María Soledad Becerril Bustamante**
Bustamante (b 1944) became the first woman elected to serve as the Commissioner of the State in 2012.

**Boabdil at the Alhambra, 1492**

# 🔟 Places of Worship

### 1 Mosque, Almonaster la Real

MAP B3 ▪ Ayuntamiento ▪ 959 14 30 03 ▪ Open 9am–8:30pm daily

Virtually unchanged for 1,000 years, this is one of Andalucía's few surviving rural mosques *(see p56)*. Inside, it has the oldest *mihrab* (Mecca-facing prayer niche) in Spain.

**Mosque, Almonaster la Real**

### 2 La Colegiata de la Asunción, Osuna

Set on a hilltop, this massive Spanish Renaissance church dominates the town *(see p96)*. Its austere façade is relieved by a fine Plateresque portal, the Puerta del Sol. The many treasures inside include five masterpieces by José de Ribera, a Crucifixion sculpture by Juan de Mesa, beautiful Renaissance ornamentation and a wonderful Baroque altarpiece.

### 3 Oratorio de San Felipe Neri, Cádiz

MAP B5 ▪ Plaza San Felipe Neri ▪ 662 64 22 33 ▪ Open 10:30am–4pm Mon–Fri, 9am–2pm Sat, 10am–noon Sun ▪ Adm

As the commemorative plaques adorning the façade reveal, this fine Baroque church is one of the most significant buildings in Spain. On 29 March 1812, Spanish patriots defied a Napoleonic blockade and met here to compose the country's first constitution.

### 4 Monasterio de San Jerónimo, Granada

MAP F4 ▪ C/Rector López Argueta 9 ▪ 958 27 93 37 ▪ Open Mar–Aug: 10am–1:30pm & 4–7:30pm daily; Sep–Feb: 10am–1pm & 3–6:30pm Mon–Sat ▪ Adm

This Renaissance magnum opus is largely the creation of Diego de Siloé, one of the great masters of the age. The façade's upper window is flanked by sinuous mythological animals and medallions. The altar is complex and monumental, consisting of row upon row of high reliefs framed by columns.

**Monasterio de San Jerónimo, Granada**

**Moorish arches inside La Mezquita**

Cristo, is brought out for the faithful to kiss. This is believed to be the cloth that St Veronica used to wipe Christ's face on the road to Calvary. A miraculous impression of the holy face is said to have been left upon it.

**8 Seville Cathedral**
The vast cathedral is Seville's most striking architectural masterpiece. It has soaring columns, precious artworks and the world's largest altarpiece (see pp18–19).

**9 Capilla Real and Catedral, Granada**
Although not without aesthetic merit, these two structures (see pp116–7) are more about Christian triumph and royal ego than they are about spirituality. At the Royal Chapel's sarcophagi, note how Queen Isabel's head presses more deeply into her marble pillow than that of King Fernando – said to indicate greater intelligence. In the Sacristy Museum, there are paintings by several 15th-century artists including Juan de Flandes and Sandro Botticelli.

**5 La Mezquita, Córdoba**
This spectacular mosque (see pp24–5) may have been savagely reconsecrated but visitors can still see its Byzantine mosaics and other exquisite marvels.

**6 Iglesia de San Mateo, Lucena**
MAP E3 ▪ Open 7:30am–1:30pm & 7–9pm daily
It's intriguing to find one of the masterpieces of Andalucían Rococo design in this industrial town – Lucena was famous for having been a virtually indepen-dent Jewish enclave during Moorish rule. The gem of this 15th-century church is its 18th-century octagonal sacristy and the decorative dome.

**7 Catedral de Jaén**
The cathedral was primarily the work of famed Renaissance architect Andrés de Vandelvira (see p127), although the west façade was designed later, decorated with Baroque sculptures by Pedro Roldán. Each Friday, at 10:30am–noon and 5–6pm, one of Spain's holiest relics, the Reliquía del Santo Rostro de

**Granada cathedral's lavish interior**

**10 Çapilla del Salvador, Ubeda**
Designed by Siloé and Vandelvira, this masterpiece of Andalucían Renaissance was commissioned as a family pantheon and is still pri-vately owned (see p35). The sacristy is the highlight, employing caryatids and atlantes as columns and pilasters. It was once embellished by a Michelangelo sculpture, a sad casualty of the Spanish Civil War.

# 📖10 Alcázares, Palacios and Castillos

## 1 Real Alcázar, Seville

This resplendent palace (see pp20–21) and extensive gardens constitute a world of royal luxury. The architectural styles are a blend of mainly Moorish traditions – note the lavish use of the horseshoe arch, glazed tilework and wood ceilings.

## 2 Palacio de las Dueñas, Seville

**MAP M1 ▪ C/Dueñas 5 ▪ Open 10am–6pm daily (summer: to 8pm) ▪ Adm ▪ www.lasduenas.es**

Built between the 15th and 16th centuries, this luxurious palace is the official city residence of the Duke of Alba. In addition to its magnificent architecture, Las Dueñas is also home to a vast collection of art and a beautiful garden.

## 3 Fortaleza de la Mota, Alcalá la Real

**MAP E3 ▪ Open Apr–mid-Oct: 10:30am–7:30pm daily; mid-Oct–Mar: 10am–6pm daily ▪ Adm**

This Moorish castle crowns the hill above the town (see p127). Created by Granada's rulers in the 8th century, it incorporates 12th-century structures and earlier elements. After the Christian reconquest in 1341 (see p42), additions to the fortress continued till the 16th century. The keep houses a visitor centre.

**Fortaleza de la Mota, Alcalá la Real**

**Decorative tiles, La Casa de Pilatos**

## 4 La Casa de Pilatos, Seville

Few palaces are more opulent than this 16th-century mansion (see p85). Featuring a mix of Mudéjar (Christian-Islamic), flamboyant Gothic and Renaissance styles, it is also adorned with Classical sculptures, including a 5th-century BCE Greek Athena and Roman works. A noble residence to this day, the mansion is filled with family portraits and antiques.

## 5 Palacio del Marqués de la Gomera, Osuna

**MAP D4 ▪ C/San Pedro 20 ▪ 954 81 26 32**

Now a hotel and restaurant, this 18th-century palace is a striking example of the Spanish Baroque style. The family escutcheon crowns the carved stone doorway.

**Palacio de Jabalquinto, Baeza**

### ⑥ Palacio de Jabalquinto, Baeza

The façade of this 15th-century palace (see p34) defies categorization, while the gallery and the patio evoke the Renaissance style.

### ⑦ Castillo de Santa Catalina, Jaén

MAP F3 ■ Open Jul–mid-Sep: 10am–2pm & 5–9pm Mon–Sat; mid-Sep–Jun: 10am–6pm Mon–Sat; Jan–Dec: 10am–3pm Sun ■ Adm (free entry 5–9pm Wed) ■ www.castillosantacatalina.es

Restored by the Christians, this 13th-century castle towers above the town and affords spectacular views.

### ⑧ Castillo de Burgalimar, Baños de la Encina

MAP F2 ■ Cerro del Cueto, Plaza de Santa María 1 ■ Tour hours vary, check website for details ■ Adm ■ www.bdelaencinaturismo.com

This Moorish castle is one of the best-preserved in Andalucía. Its horseshoe-arched main gate bears an inscription dating its construction to 967 CE. Some 14 square towers provide vistas far and wide.

### ⑨ Castillo de La Calahorra

MAP F4 ■ 958 67 70 98 ■ Open 10am–1pm & 4–6pm Wed ■ Adm

One of the few castles built after the Christian reconquest, this was also one of the first in Spain to be built in Italian Renaissance style. Despite its intimidating setting and exterior, the inner courtyard is exquisite.

**Castillo de Vélez Blanco**

### ⑩ Castillo de Vélez Blanco

MAP H3 ■ 607 41 50 55 ■ Open 10am–2pm & 4–6pm Wed–Sun (May–Sep: 5–8pm)

This has the grace of a fairy-tale castle. Unfortunately, it was gutted in the early 1900s, but a reconstruction of one of the patios gives you some idea of its original splendour.

# 🔟 Aspects of Moorish Heritage

## 1 Religious Tolerance

Although non-Muslims had to pay a special tax and wear distinctive clothing, Moorish policies towards Jews and Catholics were generally easy-going. There was greater repression after the fundamentalist Almohads came into power in the 12th century, but on the whole, the various faiths were well integrated for many centuries.

**Moses Maimonides**

## 2 Music

The Moors can be credited with the early development of the guitar *(see pp50–51)*, which they adapted from the four-stringed lute. The Middle Eastern musical forms they imported were also to have an effect later on flamenco.

## 3 Gardens

Moorish gardens make prominent use of water, which is especially important to people from a perpetually arid land. It was sprayed, channelled, made to gurgle and fall, to please the ear and eye. Jasmine, honeysuckle and roses are just a few of the many flowers the Moors brought to the region.

## 4 Philosophy

Great minds of Andalucía, such as the Moor Averroës and the Jew Maimonides, were considered among the most advanced thinkers of their age. The former almost single-handedly preserved the writings of Aristotle, while the latter's writings sought to reconcile biblical faith and reason.

## 5 Crafts

The hand-tooled leather of Córdoba, silver and gold filigree jewellery, pottery, silk and embroidered goods and inlaid creations all owe their existence to the Moors' 800-year rule.

## 6 Agriculture

Inheriting many of their techniques from the Romans, the Moors were masters of agricultural engineering. Their system consisted of three main elements: the aqueduct, the waterwheel and the irrigation channel. Thereby, they were able to cultivate vast areas, often building ingenious terracing on slopes. They also introduced many crops, including bitter oranges, lemons, almonds, rice, cotton, asparagus and mulberry trees (to feed silk-worms).

**The lush Partal gardens with their watercourses at the Alhambra**

**Moorish calligraphy, the Alhambra**

### 7 Art and Architecture

Moorish art and architecture is full of signs and symbols and often incorporates calligraphy into its designs, quoting the Koran or poetry. The point was to inspire viewers to reflect upon the unity of all things under Allah, whose power and perfection could never be equalled by the achievements of man.

### 8 Science

Moorish scientists excelled in the fields of metallurgy, zoology, botany, medicine and mathematics. Moorish inventors also developed revolutionary devices such as the astrolabe and the quadrant, both used for navigation. Arabic numerals were introduced by them, as well as algebra (from *al-jebr*, meaning "reuniting broken parts") and the algorithm.

**A brass astrolabe**

### 9 Food

The simple fare that had existed prior to the Moorish incursion – centred around olives, wheat and grapes – gave way to flavours such as almonds, saffron, nutmeg, pepper and other spices.

### 10 Language

Modern Spanish language is full of everyday terms that come from Moorish heritage – the word for "left" (*izquierda*) is almost pure Arabic, as is any word beginning with the prefix *al-* (the).

## TOP 10 MOORISH SITES

**1 Moorish Granada**
The spectacular Alhambra palace is the gem of Spain's Moorish heritage, while the adjacent Generalife offers sumptuous gardens (see pp12–15).

**2 Vejer de la Frontera**
The most Moorish of the *pueblos blancos* (see p57).

**3 La Mezquita, Córdoba**
This vast mosque (see pp24–5) marked the beginning of the Arab-Hispanic style known as Caliphal.

**4 Baños Árabes, Ronda**
These Moorish baths (see p30) feature Arabic-style horseshoe arches.

**5 Medina Azahara, Córdoba**
Sadly now in ruins, this once splendid palace (see p125) epitomized the city's glory in the 10th century.

**6 Almonaster la Real**
This village's mosque is one of Andalucía's finest, with great views from the minaret (see p98).

**7 Alcazaba, Almería**
One of the largest surviving Moorish fortresses in the region (see p119).

**8 Alcazaba, Málaga**
Remains of the original Moorish walls and tower can still be seen (see p104).

**9 Las Alpujarras**
The villages on the slopes of the Sierra Nevada (see pp38–9) retain distinctive Moorish architecture.

**10 Real Alcázar, Seville**
The front towers and gateway of Seville's royal palace (see pp20–21) retain their Moorish origins.

**Moorish tiling, Real Alcázar**

# TOP 10 Aspects of Flamenco

**Dancers performing flamenco, which is closely associated with Andalucía**

## 1 Origins
Flamenco has a rich and complex history. Undocumented until the 19th century, the dance is thought to derive from a blend of Arabic, Jewish and Roma cultures found in Andalucía. It is believed that the purest form of flamenco, known as *cante jondo*, originated from the geographical area between Cádiz, Jerez and Seville. According to Spanish folklorist Manuel García Matos, the word "flamenco" comes from a slang term meaning "flashy" or "ostentatious".

## 2 Dance
Flamenco dance is charged with intense passion and *duende* (a transcendent state of inspiration). While similarities between Middle Eastern and North African dance forms and flamenco are obvious, the rapid staccato rhythms, combined with expressive arm and hand gestures, clearly resembles traditional kathak dancing from northern India.

## 3 Song
Flamenco song is fervent, rhythmic music full of pathos and catharsis. It can be categorized into three types: *cante jondo*, a deeply emotional song of anguish and despair; *cante intermedio*, an "intermediate" song which combines elements of Spanish music styles, and *cante chico*, a light, joyful song that celebrates life.

## 4 Guitar
The six-stringed flamenco guitar can be traced back to the medieval lute. It is lighter, shallower and less resonant than a classical guitar, and can be played extremely fast. A plate below the sound hole is used for tapping out rhythms.

## 5 Cajón
In 1977, the renowned flamenco artist Paco de Lucía discovered the Peruvian cajón while on tour. A kind of box drum that creates a sound similar to that of a dancer's heel tapping the floor, it was incorporated into de Lucía's music and has become a staple of flamenco ever since.

## 6 Palmas and Pitos
*Palmas* (hand clapping) punctuates song and dance. There are two styles, *fuertes* (hard), which is used during louder pieces, and *sordas* (soft), for quieter accompaniment. *Pitos* (snapping fingers) can also mark the rhythm at specific moments.

**Journey Through the Human Body exhibition, Museo Parque de las Ciencias**

### 6 Museo Parque de las Ciencias, Granada

This dazzling science park (see p118) is home to a range of inter-active exhibitions on such topics as the human body, outer space, the environment and technology.

### 7 Museo Municipal, Antequera

This museum is located in a striking 18th-century ducal palace (see p104), which means that many of the exhibits simply cannot compete with the context. Two that do, however, are the life-size 1st-century CE Roman bronze representing a naked young man, possibly Ganymede, cupbearer to the gods, and a life-like carving of St Francis of Assisi in wood by Pedro de Mena, a 17th-century Andalucían master.

### 8 Museo de Cádiz

A Neo-Classical mansion houses Cádiz's main museum (see p27), a rich mix of archaeological treasures and fine art. The museum features artifacts from the city's ancient cultures, including jewellery, pottery and small bronzes, but most notably a pair of 5th-century BCE marble sarcophagi. Among the art are works by Zurbarán, Rubens, Murillo and Cano. An ethnological collection features pieces that high-light aspects of the city's culture.

### 9 Museo Arqueológico, Córdoba

A small 16th-century Renaissance mansion (see p23) is home to this excellent collection, highlighting the city's importance in Roman times. In fact, the mansion was built over a Roman structure and there is an ancient patio to prove it. A sculpture of the Persian god Mithras, found at Cabra, is particularly fine. Other parts of the collection focus on Iberian finds and Moorish artifacts.

**Patio of the Museo Arqueológico**

### 10 Museo Provincial de Jaén

The lower floor contains some truly extraordinary 5th-century BCE Iberian stone sculptures. Found near the town of Porcuna, in the western part of the province, they show clear influences from Greek works. Upstairs, the museum (see p127) has some fine medieval wood sculpture.

# 🔟 Art and Cultural Figures

**1 Andrés de Vandelvira**
Andrés de Vandelvira (1509–75) was the quintessential architect of the Spanish Renaissance in Andalucía. His work spanned the three major phases of the style's predominance, from ornamental Plateresque, to Italianate Classical, to austere Herrerean. He can virtually be given sole credit for the architectural treasures in the town of Úbeda and many important edifices in Baeza (see pp34–5).

**2 Francisco de Zurbarán**
The great painter (1598–1664) spent most of his life in and around Seville, where his art adorns many churches and museums. His works are noted for their mystical qualities, dramatized by striking *chiaroscuro* (light and shade) effects.

*A King of Spain* (c. 1645) by Cano

*The Apparition of Saint Peter to Saint Peter Nolasco* (1629) by Zurbarán

**3 Velázquez**
Born in Seville, Diego Rodríguez de Silva y Velázquez (1599–1660) left for Madrid in 1623 to become court painter to the king. His was the most remarkable talent of the Golden Age of Spanish painting, taking naturalism and technique to new heights. The works that remain in his home town were mostly religious commissions; his real genius lay in portraits.

**Diego Velázquez**

**4 Alonso Cano**
Architect, painter and sculptor, Granada-born Alonso Cano (1601–67) studied art and began his illustrious career in Seville before moving to Madrid, where King Philip IV appointed him as Royal Architect and Painter. He later returned to Granada, where most of his works can be seen today.

**5 Murillo**
Bartolomé Esteban Murillo (1618–82) was the most successful of the Baroque painters from Seville. He received countless commissions to produce devotional works, notably the many *Immaculate Conceptions* seen in Andalucía.

**6 Pedro Roldán**
Roldán (1624–99) was one of the chief proponents of the Spanish aspiration to combine painting, sculpture and architecture into unified works of art, such as the altarpiece in Seville's Hospital de la Caridad (see p88).

### 7 Luisa Roldán

Seville-born Luisa Roldán (1652–1706), also known as La Roldana, was the first documented female sculptor in Spain. After creating wooden sculptures and statues for the Cathedral of Cádiz, she moved to Madrid where she became the Court Sculptor to King Charles II and Philip V.

*St Ginés de la Jara by Roldán*

### 8 Manuel de Falla

Andalucían-born de Falla (1876–1946) was Spain's finest classical composer. One of his major works, *The Three-Cornered Hat*, has its roots deep in flamenco.

### 9 Picasso

Pablo Picasso (1881–1973) was born in Málaga, although he settled in France in 1909. His native land, with images of the bullfight and later of the horrors of the Franco era, featured in his work throughout his career.

**Statue of Picasso, Málaga**

### 10 Federico García Lorca

The Granada-born poet and playwright (1898–1936) was also an artist, musician and theatre director. Due to his sexuality and Socialist views, he was murdered by Franco's Nationalists at the start of the Spanish Civil War. His work shows his love for Andalucían culture.

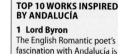

## TOP 10 WORKS INSPIRED BY ANDALUCÍA

**1 Lord Byron**
The English Romantic poet's fascination with Andalucía is chronicled in his *Don Juan* (1819).

**2 Michael Jacobs**
*Factory of Light* (2003) is a vivid, witty and informative account of life in the Andalucían village of Frailes, near Jaén.

**3 Washington Irving**
The American writer lived in Granada for some time and produced the hit *Tales of the Alhambra* (1832).

**4 Chris Stewart**
Former Genesis drummer wrote *Driving Over Lemons*, a memoir about relocating to an Andalucían farmhouse.

**5 Serafín Estébanez Calderón**
This Málaga-born writer's *Andalusian Scenes* (1847) featured the first literary description of a Roma festival.

**6 Salman Rushdie**
The Indian-born British-American author's *The Moor's Last Sigh* (1995) was inspired by the exile of Granada's last Moorish king.

**7 Manuel Machado**
The works of Machado (1874–1947), such as *Cante Jondo*, evoke a poetic passion for Andalucía.

**8 Dalí and Buñuel**
This Surrealist pair created the avant garde film *Un Chien d'Andalou* in 1928.

**9 Ernest Hemingway**
*For Whom the Bell Tolls* (1940) was based on the American writer's Andalucían experiences during Spain's Civil War.

**10 Opera**
Operas set in Andalucía include *The Marriage of Figaro* (1786, Mozart), *The Barber of Seville* (1816, Rossini) and *Carmen* (1875, Bizet).

**Scene from *The Barber of Seville***

# 🔟 Villages

(see p98) **Almonaster la Real**
From a distance, this lovely *pueblo blanco* in Huelva Province looks like a sprinkling of snow amid the green of the surrounding forests. The citadel (see p98) features one of the oldest mosques in the region, dating from the 10th century.

**Monument on the cliff above Alájar**

**2 Alájar**
Another pretty Huelva Province village (see p98), where the stone houses seem ageless. There are some nice Baroque churches too. More intriguing, however, is the mystical importance of the place, as seen in the hallowed caves and hermitage on the cliff above the town.

**3 El Rocío**
Deserted for the majority of the year, except for its handful of residents – who still customarily get around on horseback – this town (see p36) overflows with around one million pilgrims during the annual Romería. It's worth a visit at any time to take in its wonderful Wild West-style architecture, as well as to book a tour of the nearby Doñana nature reserve (see pp36–7).

**4 Cazorla**
MAP G3
Simple whitewashed cubes cluster around a citadel here, while birds of prey overhead remind you that this is the southwestern entrance to the Sierra de Cazorla (see p61). The town's position made it desirable for Moors and Christians, hence the castle in town and the ruined La Iruela, 1 km (0.5 miles) away.

**5 Arcos de la Frontera**
The historic part of this town (see p106) is from the Cuesta de Belén to the Puerta de Matrera – a zone that has been a beautifully preserved national monument since 1962. Central to the area is the Plaza del Cabildo, with ancient walls in evidence and set about with orange trees. Sadly, the castle below the square is not open to the public, but the terrace of the parador opposite is a fine place for a drink with a view.

**Narrow street in Vejer de la Frontera**

### 6 Vejer de la Frontera

This inland village *(see p107)* in Cádiz Province probably retains its quintessential Moorishness more than any other town in Andalucía. It stands gleaming white on a hill with a view of the coast, and its warren of maze-like alleys and byways is virtually indistinguishable from any North African town. Before the Spanish Civil War, women here wore a traditional veiled garment like the Muslim *hijab*, called the *cobijado*; now they are only worn during August festival.

### 7 Iznatoraf
MAP F2

This mountain eyrie of a place opens out onto 360-degree panoramas of the Cazorla highland. The best view is from the mirador above the cliff at the village's northern edge.

### 8 Zahara de la Sierra
MAP C4

The town's name means "flower" in Arabic and this quiet little hamlet *(see p105)*, scented with orange groves, lives up to its

reputation. It's a delight to see on the approach and offers fine views once there. The ruined castle, however, stands witness to tougher times. In the 15th century it was attacked continually, sought by both Muslims and Christians for its position guarding the access route to the Serranía de Ronda *(see p68)*.

### 9 Sabiote
MAP F2

This hamlet is a hidden gem, with medieval walls that are largely intact and one of the most impressive castles in the region. The castle, Moorish in origin, was restored by the famed architect Andrés de Vandelvira, who was born here.

**Restored ruins of Sabiote castle**

### 10 Castril
MAP G3

At the foot of an imposing stone outcropping and surrounded by the Parque Natural de la Sierra de Castril, this enchanting town dates back to Roman times. A mountain torrent surges below the idyllic hamlet.

**The approach to Zahara de la Sierra**

# ㄸㅁ Paseos, Plazas, Parks and Gardens

## ① Alcázar de los Reyes Cristianos, Córdoba

A major delight of Córdoba is the grounds of this fort-cum-palace dating back to the 14th century *(see p23)*. The gardens are lavishly done in Moorish style, indulging in a profusion of colour setting off the sun-bleached stone walls and ancient carvings. Another tourist attraction nearby is Baños del Alcázar Califal, the 10th-century Arab bathhouse that uses the classical order of Roman baths, with cold, warm and hot rooms.

**Alcázar de los Reyes Cristianos**

## ② Plaza San Juan de Dios, Cádiz

This is one of Cádiz's busiest hubs of commercial and social life. Lined with cafés, bars and palm trees, its chief adornment is the monumental Neo-Classical façade of the Ayuntamiento (town hall), along with several handsome towers *(see p27)*. The square opens out onto the port, ensuring a constant stream of pedestrians and opportunities for hours of people-watching.

## ③ Parque Genovés, Cádiz

**MAP B5**

Lying along the west side of Cádiz, this swathe of landscaped greenery facing the seafront has paths for strolling along, some civic sculpture and interesting flora, including an ancient dragon tree originally from the Canary Islands. This is one leg of a two-part park, the other half curving around along the northern seafront.

## ④ Jardín Botánico La Almunya del Sur, Almeria

**MAP G5** ■ Paraje Tarambana, 284 ■ 649 41 49 74 ■ Open 10am–2pm Thu–Sun (also 4–7pm Thu–Sat) ■ Adm ■ www.laalmunyadelsur.es

A lovely oasis, this botanical garden has over 1,600 types of plants spread across different biodiverse spaces. Fruit trees, ornamental trees, shrubs, vines, succulents and a range of colourful flowers line the walkways, where you'll also find water features and shaded areas to relax and take in the surroundings. Book your visit in advance.

## ⑤ Paseo Alcalde Marqués de Contadero, Seville

This central promenade is one of Seville's loveliest. Stretching along the riverfront, within sight of most of the major monuments, its tree-lined walkways make a pleasant break from the crowded city streets. The *paseo* is also pedestrianised so you don't have to worry about traffic as you stroll *(see p89)*.

**Paseo Alcalde Marqués de Contadero, Seville**

**A pavilion in Parque de María Luisa**

### 6 Jardín Botánico la Concepción, Málaga

MAP E5 ▪ Ctra N331 km 166, Málaga ▪ 951 92 61 80 ▪ Open 9:30am–5:30pm Tue–Sun (Apr–Sep: to 8:30pm) ▪ Adm ▪ www.laconcepcion.malaga.eu

Just north of Málaga lies this impressive botanical garden, the work of a 19th-century English woman, Amalia Livermore, and her Spanish husband, Jorge Loring Oyarzábal. The garden houses a collection of palms and plants from around the world. The grounds are also embellished with charming touches, such as a domed gazebo decorated with tiles and columns. Visitors can stay in the garden for half an hour after the closing time.

**Jardín Botánico la Concepción**

### 7 Plaza de la Corredera, Córdoba

MAP D3

Córdoba gave this 17th-century arcaded square a long overdue sprucing up for the tourist onslaught of 1992 (see p43), even putting in an underground car park. But it still retains some of its customary functions, including an open-air market on Saturday morning, in addition to the regular market in the building with the clock tower. The arches provide shade for cafés and tapas bars, from where you can admire the brick façades with wrought-iron balconies.

### 8 Parque de María Luisa, Seville

Seville's glorious main park was a gift to the city from a Bourbon duchess in 1893. It was redesigned for the 1929 Ibero-American Exhibition. Numerous lavish structures have been left behind, including the stunning Plaza de España (see p89) and several other fine buildings, two of which house local museums. The grounds are largely the creation of Jean-Claude Nicolas Forestier, the French landscape gardener who also designed the Bois de Boulogne in Paris.

### 9 Plaza Nueva, Granada

MAP Q2

Located at the base of both the Alhambra hill and Albaicín (see pp12–17), and providing views along the banks of the river that runs beneath the city, this is a great place to while away the time. There are street performers, and plenty of cafés with tables outside.

### 10 Paseo de la Constitución, Baeza

Baeza's hub for strollers and café-goers is this oblong central promenade that was built in the 16th century. Fountains grace its tree-lined length, and there are bars with shady seating. Interesting buildings by the square include La Alhóndiga, the former corn exchange (see p34).

# 🔟 Nature Reserves

**Limestone rock formations at El Torcal de Antequera**

## ① El Torcal de Antequera
**MAP D4**

Málaga Province's most dramatic natural sight is this limestone massif (see p79), carved by the weather over countless millennia into bizarre forms. It's a popular destination for hikers and climbers (see p107).

## ② Parque Nacional Sierra Nevada

Spain's highest mountains and Europe's southernmost ski resort can be found in this national park (see pp38–9). It's a wonderful area for hiking, horse riding and mountain biking.

## ③ Sierra de Aracena y Picos de Aroche Park

This part (see p98) of the Sierra Morena in Huelva Province is rural in character; traditions cling tighter here, notably the culinary techniques that give rise to its world-famous ham, *jamón ibérico*. The forested hills lend themselves to exploration (see p68) on foot or horseback.

## ④ Sierra Norte
**MAP C3**

Sevilla Province's northern reaches are wild and beautiful. Hiking is often a better option than driving, due to rough, pot-holed roads. A great choice for outdoor enthusiasts of any sort – anglers, hunters and climbers are in their element here.

## ⑤ Parque Nacional de Doñana

These floodplains (see pp36–7) are a UNESCO Biosphere Reserve and have been a national park since 1969, though its status is increasingly under threat due to ecological issues. More than six million birds stop here during their migrations and fauna includes the last of the Iberian lynx population.

## ⑥ Sierra de Grazalema
**MAP C5**

A huge expanse of verdant wilderness was designated a UNESCO Biosphere Reserve in 1977. Access is strictly controlled and is only possible on foot.

**Walking in the Sierra de Grazalema**

###  Cabo de Gata-Níjar
MAP H4

In Almería Province, a stretch of pristine coastline has been set aside as a nature reserve *(see p65)*, with towering rocks setting off beaches and coves. The semi-desert massif was designated a UNESCO Biosphere Reserve in 1997. The zone is excellent for scuba-diving.

###  Sierra de Cazorla
MAP G2

In eastern Jaén Province, this vast and enormously diverse park is home to some 1,300 known species of flora, including 20 that are unique to the zone. Steep cliffs, deep gorges and an intricate pattern of rivers, lakes and streams typify the terrain. The area offers plenty of walking opportunities.

**Sierra de Cazorla**

###  Parque Natural de la Sierra de Cardeña y Montoro
MAP E2

This beautiful park is home to forests of holm oak, cork and pine. For the most part gently rolling, it gives way to more dramatic topography in the west. There are plenty of hiking trails and places to spot local fauna.

### 10 Parque Natural de los Montes de Málaga
MAP E5

Most of this park was planted to cloak Málaga's once barren heights so as to prevent the seasonal flooding the city experienced for several centuries. Just 30 minutes from town, it's a fine place for hiking and biking, with colour-coded trails.

---

**TOP 10 FLORA AND FAUNA**

**Flamingos at Fuente de Piedra**

**1 Marsh birds**
Watery areas abound in cranes, flamingos, wild ducks, gull-billed terns, purple gallinules, stilts, glossy ibis and redshanks.

**2 Shrubs**
Along the coast you'll see agave, brought here from America in the 18th century. Also prickly pear, bull-rush, club rush, oleander and arbutus.

**3 Wild flowers**
Look for the Cazorla violet, bubil lily, Nevada daffodil and white celandine.

**4 Raptors**
Birds of prey include the Spanish imperial eagle, the golden eagle, griffon vultures and the peregrine falcon.

**5 Songbirds**
Listen out for the red-legged partridge, collared pratincole and hoopoe.

**6 Trees**
These include black and umbrella pine, holm oak, hazel, olive, citrus, cypress, juniper, ash and the rare Spanish fir.

**7 Mammals**
Wild creatures include wolves, lynxes, boar, genets, civets, mongoose, monk seal, dolphins, whales and the Barbary macaques of Gibraltar.

**8 Reptiles and Amphibians**
This group includes the Montpellier snake, the Spanish lizard and the natterjack toad.

**9 Fish**
Local catch includes black perch, eel, gambusia, tuna, monkfish, sardines, anchovies and cephalopods.

**10 Insects and Arachnids**
Most of Europe's butterflies are found here, along with mosquitoes, scorpions and tarantulas.

*Following pages* Hiker, El Torcal de Antequera

# ᴛᴏᴘ10 Beaches

**Playa Puerto del Mar, Almuñécar**

## 1 Almuñécar

The main resort *(see p119)* on the Costa Tropical of Granada Province is a more relaxed alternative to the intensity of the Costa del Sol. The two central beaches are the Playa San Cristóbal and the Playa Puerto del Mar, separated by a headland. Good diving and windsurfing spots can be found along here.

## 2 Mazagón
### MAP B4

Huelva Province's Costa de la Luz has several appealingly remote beaches, and Mazagón is one of them. Located 23 km (14 miles) southeast of Huelva, this low-key resort is surrounded by pines and has lovely dune beaches. Deserted in winter, it comes alive in summer, mostly with Spanish families, but there's plenty of empty expanse to find solitude.

## 3 Chipiona

Cádiz Province has some good beach resorts that lack some of the high tourism of further along the coast, and Chipiona *(see p107)* is one of the nicest. The beaches are excellent and the town has retained its age-old traditions. It's still a thriving fishing port, for example, as well as a renowned producer of the local sweet muscatel wine. In addition, historic attractions include the longest jetty in the Guadalquivir estuary, known as Turris Caepionis to the Romans and these days as Torre Scipio.

## 4 Tarifa

Cádiz Province's – and Europe's – southernmost point *(see p107)* is one of the best spots in the world for devotees of the West Wind. The wind rarely ceases blowing here, which makes it a top spot for kite- and windsurfing, but less ideal for sunbathers. Still, it is possible to find protected niches that shelter you from the wind, and the nightlife and sense of fun here are second to none.

**Windsurfing off the beach at Tarifa**

### ⑤ Marbella
**MAP D5**

The Costa del Sol's most exclusive town (see p32) naturally has several fine beaches to recommend. To the east there are Cabo Pino, a nudist beach, and Las Dunas, sand dunes beside a modern marina. To the west is a string of party beaches, good for barbecues and dancing, including Nikki beach, perhaps Marbella's best.

**A sandy beach in Marbella**

### ⑥ Torremolinos
**MAP E5**

Considering that they are in the main Costa del Sol nightlife magnet, Torremolinos's beaches come as a pleasant surprise (see p33). Because of the steep streets, most of the action remains above as you make your way down to the sand.

### ⑦ Torre del Mar
**MAP E5**

Very much off the beaten track, this area (see p33) – frequented mostly by local Spanish families – has vast sandy beaches and a fun-filled waterpark nearby.

### ⑧ Nerja
**MAP E5**

This little town (see p33) is a favourite for those who want an alternative to the brash Costa del Sol. It's a welcoming spot, with a wonderful position on top of an imposing cliff with palm-fringed beaches below.

### ⑨ Ayamonte
**MAP A4**

Andalucía's westernmost town is located at the mouth of Río Guadiana, and just to the east are the beach resorts Isla Canela and Isla Cristina. Isla Canela has a long, broad beach and an array of bars, while Isla Cristina has a fine sandy stretch and a harbour.

### ⑩ Cabo de Gata
**MAP H5**

Almería Province offers some of the finest unspoiled beaches in the region, including the Cala de la Media Luna and the Playa de Mónsul. The main resort town in this natural park (see p61) is San José.

**Playa de Mónsul, Cabo de Gata**

# ⏱🔟 Outdoor Activities and Sports

**Hiking in the Sierra Nevada mountains**

### ① Hiking
FEDAMON: 958 29 13 40; www.fedamon.com

Andalucía's sierras range from verdant to desert-like and rocky, and are perfect for hiking (see pp60–61). If mountaineering appeals, head for the Sierra Nevada. Maps and lists of refuges are available from the Federación Andaluza de Montañismo (FEDAMON).

### ② Windsurfing and Surfing
ION Club: MAP C6; 619 34 09 13; www.ion-club.net ▪ Windsurf la Herradura: MAP F5; Paseo Marítimo 34; 958 64 01 43; www.windsurf laherradura.com

Tarifa is a magnet for windsurfers, while good possibilities can also be found along the Costa Tropical. For board surfing, the Costa de la Luz provides surfers with sufficiently

**Windsurfing at Tarifa**

high waves. Mediterranean waves are the best for body-boarding or SUP (stand-up paddleboarding).

### ③ Horse Riding
Far and Ride (7 destinations in Andalucía): MAP C5; 0845 00 66 552 (from UK); +44 1462 701 110 (intnl); www.farandride.com ▪ Rutas a Caballo Castellar de la Frontera: C/ Principe Juan Carlos 30; 629 57 24 46; www.castellargp.es

Andalucía is renowned for breeding fine horses and offers a range of riding options, with trails and schools in every province.

### ④ Spelunking
MAP D5 ▪ Team4you: Avda de las Naciones Unidas, Puerto Banús, Marbella; 952 90 50 82; www.team4you.es

The region has some of the world's most interesting caves, many of them commercially developed. For information and organized jaunts, contact Team4you.

### ⑤ Skiing
Sol y Nieve ski resort near Granada is the only possibility for skiing in Andalucía. Although a little too sleek compared to its Alpine cousins, it offers a variety of runs and, best of all, skiing (see p39) fairly late in the season.

### ⑥ Boating and Fishing
Andalucían Fishing Federation: 956 18 75 85; www.fapd.net ▪ Andalucían Sailing Federation: Avda Libertad, Puerto de Santa María (Cádiz); 956 85 48 13; www.fav.es

With so many marinas along the coast, sailing is big in this part of Spain. For deep-sea and freshwater fishing, you will need to obtain a licence.

### 7 Golf

So copious are the golf courses *(see p109)* that the Costa del Sol has often been dubbed the "Costa del Golf". Courses include everything from world masterpieces, designed by top golfers, to putting greens suitable for families.

### 8 Diving

**Yellow Sub Tarifa: MAP C6; 956 68 06 80; www.divingtarifa.com** ■ **Centro de Buceo Isub: MAP H5; C/Babor 3, San José de Níjar; 950 38 00 04; www.isubsanjose.com**

Off Gibraltar are many sunken ships, while the wilds around Cabo de Gata offer the most profuse underwater life. The Costa de la Luz also has some good spots, including watersport heaven, Tarifa.

**Diving at Cabo de Gata**

### 9 Football

A national obsession, football *(fútbol)* stirs up the deepest of passions here. In season, you'll encounter it in every bar, blaring out from the TV, along with animated locals.

### 10 Hot Air Ballooning

**Glovento Sur: Cuesta de San Gregorio 25, Granada; 958 29 03 16; www.gloventosur.com**

Soar in the peaceful morning skies aboard hot air balloons, enjoying views of the Andalucían countryside.

**TOP 10 BIKE ROUTES**

**Bikers on a cycle path, Andalucía**

**1 Vía Verde El Ronquillo, Sevilla**
MAP B3
A pleasant 9-km (5.6-mile) route running along the Minilla reservoir.

**2 Vía Verde de Sierra Norte, Sevilla**
MAP C3
Ride 15 km (9.3 miles) along the Ribera del Huéznar river to Cerro del Hierro.

**3 Vía Verde of Riotinto, Huelva**
MAP B3–A4
A 35-km (21.7-mile) trail through hilly scrublands and Riotinto's Martian terrain.

**4 Vía Verde of Subbética, Córdoba**
MAP E3
Starting from Luque, take in castles and caves in a 57-km (35.4-mile) trail.

**5 Vía Verde del Aceite, Jaén**
MAP E3
Ride through rolling hills and olive groves on this 55-km (34.2-mile) route.

**6 Vía Verde Sierra de Baza, Granada**
MAP G3
Pass meadows and the village of Baza on this 16-km (9.9-mile) ride to Caniles.

**7 Vía Verde of Entre Rios, Cádiz**
MAP B4–5
Explore farmlands and dunes along the Atlantic coast in a 16-km (9.9-mile) ride.

**8 Vía the TransAndalus, Cádiz**
MAP C6–B5
This 341 km (211.8 miles) route is best experienced on a mountain bike.

**9 Vía the TransAndalus, Málaga**
MAP C5–E4
Climb through mountains and take in stunning gorges on this 214-km (132.9-mile) bike route.

**10 Villanueva del Rosario, Málaga**
MAP D4–E4
This is a 19-km (11.8-mile) child-friendly route from Camino de las Huertas.

# 🔟 Hikes and Drives

Walking through the verdant Sierra de Aracena natural park

### 1 Hike from Alájar to Linares de la Sierra
**MAP B3**

The Sierra de Aracena is defined by soaring cliffs, wooded valleys and whitewashed villages. A good 6-km (4-mile) hike along marked trails leads from Alájar to Linares, via the hamlet of Los Madroñeros. From Alájar's main square, it follows the old road, with only one steep section.

### 2 Hike around the Villages of the Southern Tahá
**MAP F4**

This hike descends south from Pitres to arrive first at Mecinilla, then along a ravine to Mecina-Fondales. From here, you take the short or long route to Ferreirola, climb up to Atalbéitar and then back to Pitres.

### 3 Hike from Rute to Iznájar
**MAP E4**

Leave Rute on the A331 south, veer left at the fork and then take the trail on the right about 500 m (550 yd) further on. This leads down to the reservoir; turn right and continue to a rocky promontory. Enjoy the views, then go up the hill and cross the bridge to the scenic village of Iznájar.

### 4 Serranía de Ronda Hike
**MAP D5**

An easy, picturesque hike connects the village of Benaoján Estación with Jimera de Líbar Estación. Begin at the Molino del Santo hotel, walk down the hill and left alongside the railway and then over it at the second crossing. Across the river is the path; when it divides, take the left fork and continue on Vía Pecuaria to town.

### 5 Drive from Nerja to Almería
**MAP E5 ▪ Rte N340**

This route takes you along some of the region's most panoramic coast-line. Nerja is built up on cliffs (see p33), and as you approach Almería the views are dramatic (see p119).

### 6 Río Borosa Hike
**MAP G2**

From the visitors' centre at the village of Torre del Vinagre, near Cazorla, this hike takes you along the narrow rock walls of the Cerrada de Elías gorge above the Río Borosa, criss-crossed by wooden bridges.

**Cerrada de Elías gorge**

##  Drive from Tarifa to Cádiz
**MAP C6 ■ Rte N340**

With immense cliffs and mammoth sand dunes, this wild sweep of the Costa de la Luz *(see p106)* is the best of the Atlantic shore. The villages of Bolonia, with its ancient Roman sites, and Vejer de la Frontera, which is steeped in Moorish heritage, both make excellent side trips.

##  Drive from Ronda to Jerez
**MAP D5 ■ Rte N342**

The attraction is the *pueblos blancos (see p105)*, in particular Grazalema, Zahara and Arcos de la Frontera, and the Roman ruins at Ronda la Vieja.

**Puente Nuevo, Ronda**

##  Drive from Guadalquivir Valley, Córdoba Province
**MAP E2**

Starting to the east of Córdoba, in the attractive hill town of Montoro, follow the river downstream. West of Córdoba, visit the once-fabulous Medina Azahara *(see p125)*, enjoy the view from Almodóvar del Río's castle walls and end at Palma del Río.

##  Drive in Las Alpujarras, Sierra Nevada
**MAP F4**

A region of villages and hamlets, many perched on the slopes of the Sierra Nevada. Begin at Lanjarón, then head for Órgiva market town. Continuing eastward, the landscape becomes more arid; eventually you will come to Yegen, made famous by Gerald Brenan's *South from Granada*.

---

**TOP 10 TOWN AND CITY WALKS**

**Córdoba's Jewish quarter**

**1 Córdoba**
Have a free-form wander around the ancient Jewish quarter and then make for the Puente Romano for sunset views *(see pp22–5)*.

**2 Granada**
Lose yourself in a maze of hilly streets in the Albaicín district *(see pp16–17)*.

**3 Seville**
Once you've done the main city-centre sights, head across the Puente de Isabel II and into the old working class quarter of Triana *(see p88)*.

**4 Cádiz**
Start at the northeast corner of Plaza de España and stroll around the city, taking in the seascapes and gardens *(see pp26–7)*.

**5 Jerez de la Frontera**
Visit the capital of sherry production and tour one of its many *bodegas (see p106)*.

**6 Ronda**
Cross the Puente Nuevo, turn left and follow the town clockwise, being sure to pass the main church *(see pp30–31)*.

**7 Baeza**
From charming Plaza del Pópulo most of the main sights are found within walking distance, in a counter-clockwise direction *(see pp34–5)*.

**8 Úbeda**
Take a westerly walk to the monumental Hospital de Santiago and the Plaza de Toros *(see pp34–5)*.

**9 Málaga**
Tour Málaga's historic sights north of the Paseo del Parque *(see p104)*.

**10 Antequera**
This ancient town's main attractions are at the foot of the Alcazaba, but enjoy the views from above *(see p104)*.

# 🔟 Children's Attractions

## 1 Muelle de las Carabelas, La Rábida, Huelva

**MAP A4** ■ Paraje de La Rábida ■ 959 53 05 97 ■ Open mid-Jun–mid-Sep: 10am–9pm Tue–Sun; mid-Sep–mid-Jun: 9:30am–7:30pm Tue–Sun ■ Closed 1 Jan, 24, 25 & 31 Dec ■ Adm (under 5s free) ■ www.muelle delascarabelasentradas.com

Down by the waterfront, the "Pier of the Caravels" is a great treat for kids (see p97). Here, they can explore the full-sized replicas of La Niña, La Pinta and La Santa María. There's also a small museum and a recreation of a 15th-century European village built around the dock.

**Replica ships, Muelle de las Carabelas**

## 2 Rio Tinto Parque Minero, Seville

Explore the 3,000 year old history of mining in the area with a visit to this museum's (see p95) reconstructed Roman mine. Children can hop on board the Rio Tinto Express for a 12-km (7.5-mile) ride to view the lunar-type landscape, old locomotives and mining equipment.

## 3 Isla Mágica, Seville

**MAP K1** ■ Pabellón España, Isla de Cartuja ■ 954 48 70 30 ■ Opening hours vary, check website for details ■ Adm ■ www.islamagica.es

This amusement park recreates the exploits of the 16th-century explorers who set out on seafaring expeditions – rides have names such as Jaguar and Anaconda. There are also boat tours and a range of shows.

## 4 Carromato de Max, Mijas

**MAP D5** ■ Avda del Compás ■ 662 18 12 56 ■ Open 10am–2pm daily ■ Adm ■ www.carromatodemijas.org

This oddball collection claims to be a compendium of the world's smallest curiosities. There's a fine copy of Da Vinci's *The Last Supper* executed on a grain of rice, fleas in suits and Churchill's head sculpted in chalk.

**Impressive mineral formations in the Cuevas de Nerja**

### 5 Cuevas de Nerja
MAP E5 ▪ Ctra Maro ▪ 952 52 95 20 ▪ Open 9:30am–4:30pm daily (Jul & Aug: to 7pm) ▪ Closed 1 Jan & 15 May ▪ Adm ▪ www. cuevadenerja.es

Discovered in 1959, these caves go back some five million years. Well-placed lighting highlights the features of each cavern, from eerie shadows to mystical waterfalls. The central column in Cataclysm Hall is the tallest in the world.

### 6 Parque de las Ciencias, Granada
MAP F4 ▪ Avenida de la Ciencia s/n ▪ 958 13 19 00 ▪ Open 10am–7pm Tue–Sat, 10am–3pm Sun & public hols ▪ Adm ▪ www.parqueciencias.com

This fascinating science centre and museum features a planetarium, a biodome holding more than 200 species of flora and fauna, inter-active exhibitions, mechanical games, workshops and optical effects sure to pique curious minds of all ages.

### 7 Aventura Amazonia, Marbella
MAP D5 ▪ Avda Valeriano Rodríguez, 2 ▪ 952 83 55 05 ▪ Opening hours vary, check website for details ▪ Adm ▪ www.aventura-amazonia.com

Aventura Amazonia is the largest adventure park in Andalucía, with 103 challenges, 24 ziplines and a daring 12 m (40 ft) "Monkey Jump". The activities are suitable for children over the age of 4.

### 8 Aqua Tropic, Almuñécar
MAP F5 ▪ Playa de Velilla, Paseo Reina Sofia ▪ 958 63 20 81 ▪ Open mid-Jun–Sep: 11am–7pm daily ▪ Adm ▪ www.aqua-tropic.com

Hours of fun, with rides called Kamikazee, Wavebreaker, Ring Rapids, Blackhole Rapids, Soft Runs and a Children's Lake for little ones.

### 9 Mini Hollywood, Almería
The Wild West rides again at this old "spaghetti western" movie set. At show time, kids can see Jesse James in action *(see p118)*.

**The streets of Mini Hollywood**

### 10 Parque Acuático Vera
MAP H4 ▪ Ctra Vera/Garrucha-Villaricos ▪ 950 46 73 37 ▪ Open mid-May–Jun & Sep: 11am–6pm daily; Jul & Aug: 11am–7:30pm daily ▪ Adm ▪ www.aquavera.com

This place will save the day when what your children need most is to cool off. There are five pools of various sizes, loads of undulating slides and tubes, as well as shaded areas.

# ⅏ Andalucían Dishes

**1 Gazpacho**

This signature Andalucían dish is a cold soup made of fresh tomatoes, green peppers, cucumber, garlic, olive oil, wine vinegar or lemon, breadcrumbs and salt. There are dozens of local variations of this nourishing refresher, which may involve almonds, grapes, melon, strawberries, red peppers and boiled egg or chopped ham garnishes. Perfect for a light lunch.

Battered *calamares* and prawns

*Tortilla española*

**2 Tortilla Española and Patatas Bravas**

Both of these dishes are ubiquitous not just in Andalucía but all over Spain. The first is a dense potato omelette with onions, fried into a savoury cake. It is served cold, by the slice, and is so filling it can make a full meal. The second consists of fried potato wedges served with a spicy tomato sauce and mayonnaise.

**3 Fish Soups**

The array of *sopas de mariscos* or *pescado* (shellfish or fish soups) seems to be limited only to the cook's imagination. Málaga favourites include *sopa viña*, a sherry-spiked version, and *cachoreñas*, with orange flavouring. Cádiz is known for its *guisos marineros* (seafood stews), made with the best seasonal fish of the region.

**4 Calamares**

All along the coast, you will encounter whole baby *calamares* (squids) served grilled – the essence of simplicity and delicious as long as they are fresh. A common alternative is to cut them into rings and batter-fry them – again, if they are fresh, they will taste sweet and tender. A complete *fritura de pescado* or *fritura mixta* (mixed fried fish) might add anchovies, prawns, chunks of cod or whatever is fresh that day.

**5 Arroz a la Marinera**

This is the Andalucían version of *paella*, an appellation that also appears on some menus. Saffron-flavoured rice is served with an assortment of fish and shellfish,

*Arroz a la marinera*

which can include prawns, clams and squid. Unlike the Valencia variety, it does not generally include sausage or chicken. The dish is also known as *arroz con mariscos*.

### 6 Monkfish

Monkfish *(rape)*, also called anglerfish, is one of the top choices for maritime eating in Andalucía. Only the tail of this unprepossessing looking fish is eaten, and it has a succulent quality similar to lobster tail or scallops. It is preferably served grilled, but can also be stewed in a rich sauce, usually tomato-based.

### 7 Tocino de Cielo

This rich egg custard pudding was traditionally made by nuns in Jerez de la Frontera.

*Tocino de cielo*, "heavenly custard"

### 8 Salads

Andalucían *ensaladas* (salads) are substantial and often include asparagus, boiled eggs, artichoke, carrots, olives, tuna and onions, in addition to lettuce and tomato.

### 9 Valle de los Pedroches

This soft sheep's cheese from Córdoba Province is typical of the regional type: strong in taste. The cheese is preserved in olive oil and enhanced with herbs.

### 10 Dessert Tarts

Cakes and sweet biscuits here typically involve Moorish ingredients such as anise, sesame, almonds and cinnamon. Most are sweetened with honey rather than sugar. Two common types are *alfajores*, with honey and almonds, and *piononos*, sometimes soaked in liqueur.

---

### TOP 10 DRINKS

**1 Mineral Water**
Choose *sin gas* (still) or *con gas* (fizzy), the best being from Lanjarón, Granada.

**2 Brandy**
Brandy is distilled in Cádiz Province, Córdoba Province and Huelva Province.

**3 Wine**
Málaga's sweet wines come from Moscatel and Pedro Ximénez grapes, while fruity Condado wines are produced from Zalema grapes.

**4 Beer**
Cruzcampo is a local, Pilsner-type *cerveza* (beer) that is popular throughout the whole of Spain.

**5 Liqueur**
Aniseed-based liqueurs come primarily from Montilla in Córdoba Province. Other liqueurs include *aguardiente* from Huelva Province and *cazalla* from Sevilla Province.

**6 Sangría**
This classic red wine punch is world famous. The lighter *Tinto de Verano* is very popular in Andalucía.

**7 Coffee**
Opt for *café solo* (espresso) or *cortado* (espresso with very little milk). *Café con leche* (coffee with milk) is drunk by Spaniards for breakfast.

**8 Mint Tea**
Granada is particularly famous for its Moroccan-style tearooms *(see p122)*, and *teterías* serving mint tea are popping up more and more.

**9 Soft Drinks**
*Refrescos* include *batidos* (milkshakes), *granizados* (iced fruit crush) and *horchata* (a milky drink made from the tuber of the tigernut plant, or *chufa*).

**10 Sherry**
The region's most famous wine *(see pp76–7)* comes from Cádiz Province.

**Sherry from the barrel**

# 🔟 Tapas Dishes

### 1 Ensaladilla
"Russian salad" is sometimes an option for vegetarians – but not for vegans, as it usually consists of diced vegetables mixed in a thick mayonnaise. Watch out, however, as there are versions with cubes of ham mixed in as well. And make sure that this, and all mayonnaise-based dishes, are freshly prepared.

### 2 Chorizo al Vino
*Chorizos* are spicy, paprika- and garlic-flavoured red sausages that can be served grilled, sautéed with wine (*al vino*), or stewed with other ingredients. They are generally made of pork. *Morcilla* (blood sausage or black pudding) is a classic country delicacy.

*Aceitunas* from Andalucía

*Chorizo al vino*

### 3 Mariscos
*Berberechos* (cockles), *almejas* (clams), *mejillones* (mussels), *pulpo* (octopus), *sepia* (cuttlefish) and *zamburiñas* (baby clams) are favourite seafood options everywhere in Spain. *Caracoles* (snails), simmered in a spicy broth, can be a rich but delicious treat.

### 4 Aceitunas
There are innumerable types of olives, from small to large, green to black, salty to sweet or whole to stuffed. The name of the dish can be confusing – although the Spanish name for the tree is the *olivo*, which comes from Latin, the word for the fruit comes from the Arabic *az-zait*, which means "juice of the olive".

### 5 Champiñones al Ajillo
Mushrooms sautéed with garlic are a regular on tapas menus. Other popular vegetable dishes include *judías* (green beans), often stewed with tomatoes and garlic, and *escalibadas* (roasted peppers) or *pisto*, the Spanish version of ratatouille.

### 6 Jamón Serrano
A complimentary slice of ham laid over the top of a *copa* (glass) is said to be how the custom of tapas (which literally means "lid") started. The finest regional type available is mountain-cured ham, but there is also *jamón york* (regular ham), as well as other cured pork products, including a local *tocino* (bacon) and *fiambres* (cold cuts). It's particularly fine when eaten with local cheese and bread, served as *tabla serrana* (plate of cured meat and cheese).

*Tabla serrana*

### 7 Albóndigas

"Meatballs" can be made from meat or fish and will most likely be stewed in a tomato sauce, together with garlic and spices. An alternative method of preparing chunks of meat, seafood or fish is by skewering them and grilling them as kebabs, either plain or spicy Moroccan-style.

### 8 Anchoas (Boquerones)

Anchovies and sardines are commonly served lightly fried in batter, but can just as likely be offered marinated and preserved in oil, or with a tomato sauce. You generally eat them minus the head but with all the bones.

*Anchoas*

### 9 Croquetas

Meat, fish or vegetables and mashed potatoes are mixed with béchamel and deep-fried to create these croquettes. A variation of this are *soldaditos* (fritters), which are made of vegetables, chicken or fish.

*Croquetas*

### 10 Alioli

This is mayonnaise laced with garlic and is served as a dish in its own right, for dipping bread into or as a condiment. Another popular relish is *pipirrana*, a compote made of tomato, onion and pepper.

---

**TOP 10 TAPAS PREPARATION STYLES**

**A selection of tapas and bread**

**1 On Bread**
Many tapas don't really come to life until applied to bread. Some are served already perched on a slice.

**2 Marinated**
Anchovies, sardines and seafood all come marinated. You'll see them sitting out on bars, possibly under glass, steeped in olive oil.

**3 Cured**
The hams of Andalucía are lightly salted – mountain-cured are the best.

**4 With Mayonnaise**
Any dish can be an excuse to slather on the *alioli*. Two dishes that often have mayonnaise are *patatas alioli* and *ensaladilla*.

**5 Pickled**
Mixed in with olives, you'll often find miniature gherkins, and possibly pearl onions, bits of garlic and hot peppers.

**6 Egg-Based**
Eggs are essential in *tortilla* (see p72) or come hard-boiled as a garnish.

**7 Fried**
Almost anything you can think of will turn up *frito* (batter-fried or sautéed), from fish to mushrooms.

**8 Grilled or Roasted**
If you want to ingest a little less oil, *a la plancha* (grilled) and *asado* (roasted) are the options to choose.

**9 Stewed**
*Estofado* variations include fish, meat, potato and vegetables, often cooked in tomato sauce.

**10 A la Marinera**
This technique, commonly used for fish and seafood, is similar to poaching and involves wine, garlic and parsley.

# Bodegas and Wineries

**Barrels of sherry fill the impressive Moorish cellars at Bodegas Fundador**

## ① Bodegas Fundador

MAP B5 ▪ Calle Puerta de Rota s/n, Jerez de la Frontera ▪ Enotourism Department: 956 15 15 52 ▪ Tour timings vary, check website for details ▪ Adm ▪ www.bodegasfundador.site

One of the most legendary of the names associated with sherry, this company was founded in 1730. A tour of the famous Moorish-style cellar "de la Ina" is *de rigueur* when in Jerez (see p106).

**Family-run González-Byass**

## ② González-Byass

MAP B5 ▪ C/Manuel María González 12, Jerez ▪ 956 35 70 16 ▪ Tour timings vary, check website for details ▪ Adm ▪ www.tiopepe.com

Although most of the main sherry producers are now largely owned by British multinationals, encouragingly, this *bodega* was bought back by the family. Founded in 1835, González-Byass's operation has two historic cellars, as well as the original tasting room.

## ③ Osborne Bodega

MAP B5 ▪ C/Los Moros, El Puerto de Santa María, Cadiz ▪ 956 86 91 00 ▪ Tours by appt ▪ Adm ▪ www.osborne.es

The black bull seen on Andalucían roadside hills is the symbol of this venerable sherry and brandy maker and a part of regional heritage.

## ④ Sandeman

MAP B5 ▪ C/Pizarro 10, Jerez de la Frontera ▪ 956 15 15 52 ▪ Tour and tasting timings vary, check website for details ▪ Adm ▪ www.sandeman.com

The distinctive silhouetted figure of The Don, in a black cape and wide-brimmed hat, dates from 1928 and is one of the first trademark images ever created. Sandeman was founded in London in 1790.

## ⑤ Bodegas Robles, Montilla

MAP D3 ▪ Ctra N331 Córdoba-Málaga km 47 ▪ 609 13 11 11 ▪ Tours by appt ▪ www.bodegasrobles.com

This organic wine producer employs an old system called *solera*, in which young wines are blended with older ones, until they mature.

## ⑥ Bodegas Alvear, Montilla

What distinguishes the wines here (see p126) is two-fold. Giant terracotta containers (*tinajas*) are sunk into the ground to keep the contents at a constant temperature, while the hot climate ripens the grapes for a stronger wine.

### 7 Bodegas Málaga Virgen
MAP D4 ▪ A-92 km 132, Finca Vistahermosa, 29520 Fuente de Piedra, Málaga ▪ 952 319 454 ▪ Tours by appt ▪ www.bodegasmalagavirgen.com
Producing traditional Málaga wines of the finest quality, this *bodega* has remained in the same family for four generations (see p104).

### 8 Bodegas Antonio Barbadillo
MAP B5 ▪ Calle Sevilla 6, Sanlúcar de Barrameda ▪ 956 38 55 21 ▪ Open 11am–3pm Tue–Sat by appt ▪ Adm ▪ www.barbadillo.com
A family-owned winery with 5 sq-km (2 sq-miles) of vineyards, the largest cellars in Sanlúcar and a museum on wine making. Barbadillo launched its first *manzanilla* in 1827 and now produces a range of wines, including one of Spain's best whites.

**Bodegas Antonio Barbadillo**

### 9 Bodegas Andrade
MAP B4 ▪ Av de la Coronación 35, Bollullos Par del Condado, Huelva ▪ 959 41 01 06 ▪ Tours by appt ▪ www.bodegasandrade.es
This *bodega* was one of the first to realize the potential of the Zalema grape for creating young wines.

### 10 Agroalimentaria Virgen del Rocío
MAP B4 ▪ Av Cabezudos 3, Almonte, Huelva ▪ 959 40 61 46 ▪ Tours by appt ▪ www.raigal.es
A series of fermenting vats form an underground cellar, where the Zalema grape is used to produce one of the region's few sparkling wines, Raigal.

## TOP 10 SHERRIES AND WINES

**Andalucían sherry**

**1 Fino**
Clear, crisp and dry, with an aroma of almonds, *fino* sherry is served chilled as an aperitif.

**2 Manzanilla**
The *fino* sherry made in Sanlúcar de Barrameda, Cádiz Province. It is dry, pale and slightly salty.

**3 Oloroso**
The layer of flor yeast is thin, or absent, as a *fino* ages, allowing partial oxidation. *Oloroso* is a rich amber, with an aroma of hazelnuts.

**4 Amontillado**
Midway between a *fino* and an *oloroso*. The layer of flor yeast is allowed to die off, so it gets darker in colour.

**5 Palo Cortado**
This has an aroma reminiscent of an *amontillado*, while its colour is closer to *oloroso*.

**6 Cream Sherry**
This international favourite results when you take an *oloroso* and sweeten it by mixing in a measure of Pedro Ximénez wine.

**7 Pedro Ximénez**
This naturally sweet wine, when aged with care, is elegant and velvety.

**8 Brandy de Jerez**
Produced only in Jerez, it is sweeter and more caramelized than French brandy. It is made by ageing wine spirits in casks that have previously been used to age sherry.

**9 Málaga**
Málaga's famous sweet wines are made from the Moscatel and Pedro Ximénez grape varieties.

**10 Raigal**
One of Andalucía's few sparkling wines, this is refreshing on the palate.

# 🔟 Andalucía for Free

**①  Archivo General de Indias, Seville**

The UNESCO-listed archives building *(see p88)* was commissioned by Philip II in 1573 as a merchant's exchange and designed by architect Juan de Herrera (who worked on El Escorial). It contains more than 80 million documents, including letters sent by Columbus to his royal patrons, Ferdinand and Isabella.

**②  Cathedral, Seville**

Normally you pay to wander around the magnificent 15th-century cathedral *(see pp18–9)*, set on the rectangular base of an Almohad mosque, but services here are free. There are choral masses at 8:30am daily from October to May.

**③  El Mirador de San Nicolás, Granada**

Go up to this high plaza to see a panoramic view of the Alhambra and surrounding districts and, on clear days, the peaks of the Sierra Nevada *(see p17)*. It's a short walk up the hill from Plaza Nueva through the winding cobblestone alleys of the Albaicín area. There are hop-on, hop-off buses for those with limited mobility.

**④  Patios, Córdoba**
MAP D3

Since Roman and Moorish days, Córdoba citizens have

**Pretty patio in Córdoba**

used their inner courtyards to catch up or take in the air during summer. Many of the oldest are in the Alcázar Viejo district, between the Alcázar and San Basilio. There are more in Santa Marina, around the church of San Lorenzo and near la Magdalena, and in Judería. Guides take groups on tours but you may explore those open to the public for yourself. At the beginning of May, for 12 days, Córdoba celebrates the Fiesta of the Patios – an event included on UNESCO's Intangible Heritage list since 2012.

**⑤  Torre del Oro, Seville**

This 12-sided military watchtower built by the Almohad dynasty in the 13th century was used to control access to Seville via the Guadalquivir river and later became a prison *(see p85)*. Its golden sheen comes from its building materials – mortar, lime and pressed hay – reflected in the river. Visitors can enter for free on Mondays.

**Torre del Oro, Seville**

### 6 Street Art, Granada

Far removed from the ancient artistic wonders of the Alhambra, Granada's side streets and walls provide rough canvases for designs by talented street artists. Some are inspired by abstract expressionist painter José Guerrero, and much of the work is witty as well as gritty.

### 7 Centro de Arte Contemporáneo, Málaga

MAP Q6 ■ C/Alemania ■ 952 20 85 00 ■ www.cacmalaga.eu

The CAC has a permanent display of international artists including pieces by Louise Bourgeois, Olafur Eliasson, Thomas Hirschhorn and Damian Hirst, as well as post-1980s Spanish art, plus rotating temporary shows.

### 8 Fundación Picasso Casa Natal, Málaga

MAP R4 ■ Plaza de la Merced 15 ■ 951 92 60 60 ■ www.fundacion picasso.malaga.eu

The birthplace museum of Picasso, housing an array of his art, is free on Sundays between 4pm and 8pm.

**Roman theatre, Ruinas de Acinipo**

### 9 Ruinas de Acinipo, near Ronda

MAP D5 ■ Ctra Ronda-Sevilla km 22 ■ 952 18 71 19

Founded in 45 BCE to house retired soldiers from the Roman legions, the Acinipo ruins include a Roman theatre that is still in use today.

### 10 El Torcal de Antequera

Known for its striking limestone rock formations, El Torcal offers excellent hiking terrain (see p107). There are three marked routes taking from 30 minutes to three hours.

---

**TOP 10 BUDGET TIPS**

**Tapas, free with a drink**

**1** In Granada – city and province – tapas still come free with a drink in most bars. The custom extends to some bars in Almería and Jaén province.

**2** At lunch, ask for the "menú del día" (daily special). It is often as little as €7 and can be a two- or three-course meal.

**3** If going out for drinks, order house wine or beer on tap over pricey cocktails.

**4** When booking trains, research low-cost options through operators Iryo or Renfe. Renfe offers free passes and discounts that can be applied to age groups and those travelling in numbers.

**5** Buy a tourist pass (bono turístico). The Granada Card, Málaga Card and Sevilla Card cover public transport and offer discounts or free entry to sights. Prices vary. Jaén, Úbeda, Baeza and Ronda also have discount bonos.

**6** Be conscientious in Marbella; prices are much higher than elsewhere.

**7** If you are a visitor from outside the EU and are leaving with purchased goods to the value of €90.15 or more, get a refund on Spain's 21 per cent sales tax (VAT, known here as IVA).

**8** Avoid the tourist-heavy flamenco shows in Seville and aim instead for bars and clubs in Triana and places where talented singers perform for local people.

**9** Don't go near any of the major cities around Easter Week (Semana Santa). Room rates can go through the roof, especially at the smarter hotels. August can also be an expensive month.

**10** Consider camping, especially if walking in Grazalema, the Alpujarra or Sierra Nevada. The sites tend to be at a high altitude and so relatively cool and pleasant, even in summer. Prices start at €5 per night per tent.

# 🔟 Religious Festivals

### ① Fiesta de los Reyes Magos
**5 Jan**

Traditionally, this evening commemorates the arrival of the Three Kings at the infant Jesus's manger crib. Parades across the region feature the trio, lavishly dressed, progressing through towns in small carriages drawn by tractors or horses. The next day, Epiphany, is the day that children receive gifts.

**Revellers celebrating at Carnaval**

### ② Carnaval
**Feb**

Most Andalucían towns celebrate this Catholic festival (see p27), the most spectacular extravaganza being in Cádiz. Costumes and masked balls are the order of the day and night during these chaotic revels. The implicit anarchy invites every sort of political lampoon, which is why Franco tried to abolish these events.

### ③ Semana Santa
**Easter week**

Holy Week is observed in every town and village in the region, with dramatic and spectacular processions, especially in Seville (see p19). Effigies of Christ and the Virgin are carried through the streets on huge floats. Dressed in traditional outfits, people either maintain penitential silence or express commiseration with the suffering Lord and His mournful Mother.

### ④ Romerías
**May–Oct**

Taking part in one of these local festivals is an experience no visitor will forget – almost every community (see p19) has its own romería. Usually, the programme involves a colourful pilgrimage to a shrine outside of town, followed by days of merrymaking. The name may recall ancient pilgrimages, when devotees walked to Rome.

### ⑤ Corpus Christi
**Dates vary**

This festival celebrates the miracle of Transubstantiation, when the Host becomes the body of Christ and the wine, His blood. Granada's celebration is the most famous, with parades and partying, followed by bullfights and flamenco.

**Corpus Christi procession**

### 6 Fiesta de las Cruces
3 May

The Festival of the Crosses celebrates the discovery of the True Cross by St Helena in the 4th century. Modes of veneration vary widely in the region, but may include competitions for producing the most gorgeous flower-decked cross.

### 7 San Juan
23 & 24 Jun

This feast, in celebration of John the Baptist, is important in many parts of Andalucía. Midsummer fireworks and bonfires seem to be the order of the day in most communities.

### 8 Virgen del Carmen
15 & 16 Jul

The patron saint of sailors is all-important in coastal communities. Statues of the Virgin are put onboard a flower-adorned fishing boat and floated out to sea and back again, amid music, fireworks and cheering.

**Virgen del Carmen festival**

### 9 Assumption of the Virgin
15 Aug

At the height of the summer heat, the Virgin Mary's assumption into heaven is celebrated. There is much socializing, drinking and dancing. The day marks the beginning of the Feria de Málaga, a week-long party.

### 10 Fiesta de San Miguel
Last week Sep–first week Oct

This mix of bullfights, exhibitions and dancing is particularly note-worthy in Seville, Úbeda and the Albaicín quarter of Granada. In Torremolinos, it closes the summer season in festive style.

---

**TOP 10 FERIAS AND OTHER FESTIVALS**

**Dancers performing flamenco**

**1 Flamenco Festivals**
Summer months
These take place around the region.

**2 Moros y Cristianos**
Throughout the year
Festivals centre on re-enactments of Christian take-overs of various towns.

**3 Feria de Abril**
Apr/May
Held in Seville two weeks after Easter, this is the largest fair *(see p86)* in Spain.

**4 Wine Festivals**
Apr–Sep
Celebrations of the fruit of the vine with *La Vendimia* (grape harvest).

**5 Feria del Caballo**
May
This fair in Jerez de la Frontera centres on Andalucían horses.

**6 Music and Dance Festivals**
Jun–Jul
Granada hosts many such festivals.

**7 Feria de Jamón**
15 Aug
This foodie festival celebrates ham cutting and hosts activities including scavenger hunts. There's also live music.

**8 Sherry Festivals**
Sep–Oct
The towns of the "Sherry Triangle" *(see p106)* celebrate their fortified wines at various times, notably in Jerez.

**9 Fiesta de la Aceituna**
1st week Dec
The olive is celebrated in the Jaén Province town of Martos.

**10 Fiesta de los Verdiales**
28 Dec
In Málaga Province at Puerta de la Torre, this is a day for practical jokes and a chance to wear funny hats. It dates back to Moorish times.

# Top 10 Andalucía and the Costa del Sol Area by Area

The Roman Bridge crossing the
Río Guadalquivir in Córdoba

# ᴛᴏᴘ➓ Seville

Andalucía's capital is an aristocratic yet relaxed city, with a fabulous cultural heritage that dates back beyond recorded history.

**Mudéjar-style tiles at La Casa de Pilatos**

Its fate has always been tied to the Río Guadalquivir ("the great river" in Arabic), and the trade it offered the city. Today, much of the riverfront is made up of an attractive promenade. There is a wealth of art and architecture to see in the historic centre of Seville as well as distinctive neighbourhoods, each with their own charm. But its highlights, including the splendid cathedral, Moorish and Renaissance palaces and fine museums, are within walking distance of each other.

**SEVILLE**

**❶** Top 10 Sights
see pp85–7

**①** Places to Eat
see p93

**①** Shops and Markets
see p90

**①** Tapas Bars and Nightlife see p92

**①** Flamenco and Theatre Venues see p91

**①** The Best of the Rest
see p88

**①** Parks, Paseos and Plazas see p89

0 metres 500
0 yards 500

**River view of the Torre del Oro**

## 1 Torre del Oro and Torre de la Plata

MAP L4 ▪ Torre del Oro: Paseo de Colón; 954 22 24 19; Open 10am–2pm Mon–Fri, 11am–2pm Sun & hols; adm €3 (except Mon) ▪ Torre de Plata: C/Santander 15 ▪ Closed to public

Tradition states that the imposing 13th-century Moorish dodecahedral (12-sided) watchtower, the Torre del Oro (Tower of Gold), is named after the golden tiles that once adorned it. Others say its name derives from its use as a warehouse for the gold coming in from the Americas during Seville's heyday. It now houses a small maritime museum. Nearby stands the Torre de Plata (Tower of Silver), a more modest octagonal tower, which most likely gets its name as a complement to its neighbour. Both towers originally formed part of the city's defences.

## 2 Real Fábrica de Tabacos

MAP M5 ▪ C/San Fernando 4 ▪ 954 55 11 23 ▪ Open 8am–8:30pm Mon–Fri ▪ Guided tours by appt; call ahead

A part of Seville University, this stately 18th-century edifice is the second-largest building in Spain. Famous for its fun-loving workers, who at one time rolled three-quarters of Europe's cigars, the old factory has been immortalized by *Carmen*, the most popular opera in the world. The doomed heroine, a hot-blooded gypsy *cigarrera*, remains, for many, a symbol of Spanish passion.

## 3 Ayuntamiento

MAP L3 ▪ Plaza Nueva 1 ▪ 955 47 02 64

This building has been the town hall since the 16th century. Inside, the rooms are decorated with historic paraphernalia of the city and the monarchy, in a blend of Gothic and Renaissance styles. Outside, the façades reflect the evolution of taste, from the original Renaissance Plateresque work with its finely carved stonework, to the 19th-century attempt to copy the style, seen from Plaza de San Francisco. In front of the building is Plaza Nueva, which hosts regular outdoor markets.

## 4 La Casa de Pilatos

MAP N3 ▪ Plaza de Pilatos 1 ▪ 954 22 52 98 ▪ Open 9am–6pm daily (Apr–Oct: to 7pm) ▪ Adm ▪ www.fundacionmedinaceli.org

Erroneously said to be based on the house of Pontius Pilate in Jerusalem, this 15th-century gem (see p46) is the most sumptuous of Seville's urban mansions. It is a blend of Mudéjar, Gothic and Renaissance styles, punctuated with Classical statuary and *azulejo* (Spanish painted ceramic tile) designs. Look for the carved head of the Greek boy, Antinous, who drowned and was deified by his grief-stricken lover, Emperor Hadrian.

**Courtyard passage, La Casa de Pilatos**

### 5 Monasterio de la Cartuja de Santa María de las Cuevas

**MAP J1** ■ Centro Andaluz de Arte Contemporáneo: 955 03 70 70; open 11am–9pm Tue–Sat, 10am–3:30pm Sun; adm; www.caac.es

This 15th-century monastery has had its ups and downs over the centuries. During Spain's age of prosperity, it was the favoured retreat of Christopher Columbus, whose remains were interred here for several decades. The monks went on to decorate their vast enclave with commissions from some of Seville's greatest artists – most of the works are now in the Museo de Bellas Artes (see p87). In 1841, it became a ceramics factory. Finally, the complex came to house a contemporary art museum, Centro Andaluz de Arte Contemporáneo.

**Museo Arqueológico**

### 6 Museo Arqueológico

**MAP N6** ■ Plaza de America ■ 955 12 06 32 ■ Closed for renovations until 2025 ■ Adm

This Renaissance-style pavilion, designed by architect Anibal González, was also one of the fabulous structures created for the 1929 Exposition and now houses Andalucía's principal archaeological museum. The assemblage of artifacts ranges from Paleolithic finds, exhibited in the basement, to splendours of Roman and Moorish art displayed upstairs. The Carambolo treasures of Tartessian gold, also on display in the basement, and the Roman sculpture collection are outstanding.

**Water tanks under the Real Alcázar**

### 7 Real Alcázar

This lavish palace (see pp20–21) was primarily the brainchild of Pedro I, who had it built as a lavish love-nest for himself and his mistress, María de Padilla.

### 8 Seville Cathedral and La Giralda

Legend has it that when the *sevillanos* decided to build their cathedral in the 15th century, they intended to erect an edifice so huge that later generations would call it outrageous. They achieved their aim with the largest church (see pp18–19) (by volume) in Christendom.

**FERIA DE ABRIL**

The seven-day Spring Fair (**below**), about two weeks after Easter, is a riot of colour and high spirits. Andalucían horses strut on parade, ridden by *caballeros* in traditional leather chaps, waistcoats and wide-brimmed *sombreros cordobeses*, often with women in flamenco attire perched behind. The air is alive with music, the fairgrounds overflow with *casetas* (party marquees – most of them by invitation only), and partying continues until dawn. All festivities take place south of the river.

## 9 Plaza de España
MAP N6

This semicircular plaza was designed as the centrepiece for the Ibero-American Exposition of 1929. Almost completely covered with gorgeous glazed tiles, its surfaces depict historic moments and heraldic symbols of the 40 regions of Spain. A canal follows the arc of the structure, crossed by colourful footbridges. The site was used as a set in the film *Star Wars: Attack of the Clones*, for its other-worldly feel.

**Gallery, Museo de Bellas Artes**

## 10 Museo de Bellas Artes
MAP K2 ▪ Plaza del Museo 9 ▪ 955 54 29 42 ▪ Open Aug: 9am–3pm Tue–Sat; Sep–Jul: 9am–9pm Tue–Sat, 9am–3pm Sun ▪ Adm (free for EU members)

This museum *(see p52)*, second only to the Prado in Madrid, houses a range of great Spanish paintings. The collection is on display in a former 17th-century convent and focuses on the Seville School, led by Cano, Zurbarán, Valdés Leal and Murillo. Look out for Murillo's touching *Virgen de la Servilleta*. Don't miss El Greco's poignant portrait of his son and the polychrome terracotta of St Jerome by Florentine sculptor Pietro Torregiano, who was a colleague of Michelangelo.

**A WALK AROUND THE BARRIO DE SANTA CRUZ**

### MORNING

Start at the exit to the **Real Alcázar** *(see pp20–21)* on Patio de las Banderas. Turn right to find the Arco de la Judería, a covered alleyway that leads to the Callejón del Agua, running along the old Jewish Quarter's southern wall. Peep into some of the famously lush patios of these perfectly whitewashed houses – the writer Washington Irving once stayed at No. 2. After the wall ends, find the **Jardines de Murillo** *(see p89)* on your right, and enjoy a tranquil stroll.

Turn back to find **Plaza Santa Cruz** *(see p89)*, where the church that gave the neighbourhood its name once stood, until it was burned down by the French in 1810. A 17th-century wrought-iron cross stands here now. Cross a couple of streets west to find the **Hospital de los Venerables** *(see p88)*. Take in its delightful central courtyard and important art gallery.

For lunch, try traditional tapas at the old **Casa Plácido** *(see p93)*.

### AFTERNOON

From here, go east to Calle Santa Teresa 8, the former home of the great artist Bartolomé Murillo *(see p54)*, who died here in 1682 after a fall while painting frescoes in Cádiz.

Finally, work your way back towards the **cathedral** *(see pp18–19)* along Calle Mesón del Moro and then to Calle Mateos Gago. At No 1 you'll find the **Cervecería Giralda** *(954 22 82 50)*, excellent for a drink or food at any time of day.

*See map on p84* ←

# The Best of the Rest

Valdés Leal frescoes, Hospital de los Venerables

## ① Hospital de los Venerables

MAP M4 ▪ Plaza de los Venerables 8 ▪ Open 10am–7pm Mon–Sat, 10am–3pm Sun ▪ Adm ▪ www.fundacion focus.com

Founded in the 17th century as a home for the elderly, this is now a cultural centre. It features a *trompe-l'oeil* ceiling by Juan de Valdés Leal.

## ② Archivo General de Indias

MAP M4 ▪ Avda de la Constitución 3 ▪ 954 50 05 28 ▪ Open 9:30am–4:30pm Mon–Sat, 9:30am–1:30pm Sun

This is a storehouse for documents on the Spanish colonization of the Americas *(see p78)*.

## ③ Museo de Artes y Costumbres Populares

MAP N6 ▪ Plaza de América 3 ▪ 955 54 29 51 ▪ Open 9am–9pm Tue–Sat (16 Jun–15 Sep: to 3pm), 9am–3pm Sun ▪ Adm

Exhibits here include displays on flamenco and bullfighting.

## ④ Hospital de la Caridad

MAP L4 ▪ C/Temprado 3 ▪ Open 10am–7pm Mon–Fri, 2–7pm Sat & Sun ▪ Adm (free 3:30–7pm Mon) ▪ www.santa-caridad.es

A hospital founded by reformed rake Miguel de Mañara. The chapel contains artworks by Sevillian artists.

## ⑤ Real Maestranza

MAP L3 ▪ Paseo de Cristóbal Colón 12 ▪ Open 9:30am–9:30pm daily (Apr–Oct: to 9pm) ▪ www.realmaestranza.es

The so-called "Cathedral of Bullfighting" becomes the focal point of Seville when the sporting season opens in April.

## ⑥ Barrio de Triana

MAP K4

This quarter was known for producing bullfighters, flamenco artists and fine ceramics *(see p90)*.

## ⑦ Casa de la Condesa de Lebrija

MAP M2 ▪ C/Cuna 8 ▪ 954 22 78 02 ▪ Open 10am–6pm daily (Jul–Aug: Mon–Sat) ▪ Adm

A 15th-century, typically Sevillian mansion, embellished with mosaics from Itálica *(see p97)*.

## ⑧ Museo de las Ilusiones

MAP M1 ▪ Calle San Eloy 28 ▪ 955 66 98 39 ▪ Open 10am–10pm daily ▪ Adm ▪ www.moisevilla.es

An infinity room, an anti-gravity room and a vortex tunnel are some of the highlights at this museum of illusions.

## ⑨ La Macarena

MAP N1

This district is home to the Rococo Iglesia de San Luis, the 15th-century Convento de Santa Paula, and Seville's adored religious icon, the Virgen de la Macarena. During Semana Santa *(see p80)* she is paraded on a float.

## ⑩ Museo del Baile Flamenco

MAP M3 ▪ C/Manuel Rojas Marcos 3 ▪ 954 34 03 11 ▪ Open 12:30–6pm daily ▪ Adm ▪ Daily shows from 7pm

Run by famous dancer Cristina Hoyos, this museum explores the wonderful world of flamenco dancing.

# Parks, Paseos and Plazas

**1 Real Alcázar**
These gardens are a blend of Moorish and Italian Renaissance styles *(see pp20–21)*.

**2 Plaza Santa Cruz**
MAP N4
Created when Napoleon's soldiers destroyed a church that stood here, this square is now adorned by an iron cross, La Cruz de la Cerrajería.

**3 Plaza de San Francisco and Plaza Nueva**
MAP L3 & M3
These squares represent the heart of the city. Plaza de San Francisco (also the Plaza Mayor, or main square) is Seville's oldest and hosts many public spectacles. Plaza Nueva is a pleasant park with a monument to King Fernando the Saint.

**4 Jardines de Murillo**
MAP N4
These formal gardens used to be the orchards and vegetable plots for the Alcázar. Donated to the city in 1911, they are named after Seville painter Bartolomé Murillo *(see p54)*. The Columbus monument features the bronze prows of the *Santa María*, the caravel that bore him to the Americas in 1492.

**5 Parque de María Luísa**
MAP M6
This park dominates the southern end of the city. Its present design, comprising the immense Plaza de España, was laid out for the 1929 Exposition *(see p59)*. Look for peacocks in the trees.

**Parque de María Luísa**

**6 Plaza de la Encarnación**
MAP M2
This square is dominated by the intriguing architecture of the Metropol Parasol complex, with its shops, bars, observation deck, market and subterranean museum.

**Plaza de la Encarnación**

**7 Alameda de Hércules**
MAP M1
Set off by pairs of columns at either end – the southern set are ancient Roman – this popular promenade is lined with trendy bars and restaurants, which draw a hip crowd.

**8 Plaza de la Alfalfa**
MAP M2
Once the location of the hay market, and later a Sunday morning pet market, the Alfalfa is now a good area for browsing. Visit clothing stores, flamenco boutiques, unique accessory shops and bars.

**9 Paseo Alcalde Marqués de Contadero**
MAP L4
With the Torre del Oro at one end *(see p85)*, this riverfront walkway makes for a pleasant stroll *(see p58)*.

**10 Calle San Fernando and Avenida de la Constitución**
MAP M5
These two streets form a pedestrian promenade through the heart of Seville, livened up by art exhibitions.

*See map on p84*

# Shops and Markets

### ① El Corte Inglés
MAP L2 ▪ Plaza del Duque
de la Victoria 8

Although you're unlikely to find any bargains here, the range of merchandise is impressive. Spain's main department store chain carries not only clothes and accessories, but also perfume, housewares and sporting goods. There's also a gourmet food section and food hall, as well as a supermarket.

**Pottery on sale at the Ceramica Triana**

### ② Ceramica Triana
MAP J4 ▪ C/Callao 14
▪ 954 33 21 79

The place to buy the famous Triana pottery, this shop sells everything from replicas of 16th-century tiles to ashtrays. The old ceramics factory next door is now a museum.

### ③ La Guarnicioneria Lopez
MAP M3 ▪ C/Cuna 34 ▪ 954
21 69 23

For quality handmade leather goods, from wallets and handbags to equestrian gear and fashionable accessories, this is the place to go.

### ④ Massimo Dutti
MAP L2 ▪ C/Velázquez 12
▪ www.massimodutti.com

Fashionable and timeless designs for men and women can be found at this famous Spanish chain.

### ⑤ Aurora Gaviño
MAP M3 ▪ C/Álvarez Quintero
16 ▪ 628 24 56 26

This is a good spot to splurge on all the flouncy dresses, mantillas, shawls and so forth that are needed to participate in the various festivals (see pp80–81) that abound in the region.

### ⑥ Art Market
MAP K2 ▪ Plaza del Museo 9

On Sunday mornings from around 9am to 2pm, local artists display their works. Take home an original souvenir of Seville.

### ⑦ Botellas y Latas
MAP M1 ▪ C/Regina 14
▪ 954 29 31 22

This wine merchant and delicatessen has a large selection of excellent Spanish wines and gourmet regional produce. Carlos, the owner of this establishment, is very welcoming.

### ⑧ El Mercadillo
MAP M1 ▪ C/Feria 43
▪ Open 8am–3pm Thu

Just off the Alameda de Hércules (see p89), the eclectic Mercadillo El Jueves flea market is Seville's most famous second-hand market. It consists mostly of old junk, books and posters. Still, it's fun to look for the occasional treasure.

### ⑨ Hippy Market
MAP L2 ▪ Plaza del Duque
de la Victoria ▪ Open 9am–8:30pm
Wed–Sat

This is the place to find handmade jewellery, leather goods, unique clothes and other charming hand-crafted items.

### ⑩ Torre Sevilla Shopping Centre
MAP J2 ▪ C/Gonzalo Jiménez de Quesada 2

This open-air shopping centre offers an abundance of high-street shops and restaurants.

→ See map on p84

# Flamenco and Theatre Venues

**Performance, Teatro de la Maestranza**

## 1 Teatro de la Maestranza
MAP L4 ■ Paseo de Cristobal Colón 22 ■ 954 22 33 44 ■ www.teatrodelamaestranza.es

Built as part of Expo '92, Seville's main theatre serves primarily as the city's opera house, with productions of all the classics, particularly those set in Seville, including *Carmen*, *Don Juan* and *The Barber of Seville*.

## 2 Casa de la Memoria de al-Andalus
MAP M2 ■ C/Cuna 6 ■ 954 56 06 70 ■ Hours vary, check website for details ■ www.casadelamemoria.es

Dedicated to flamenco, this cultural centre hosts exhibitions, concerts and dance performances.

## 3 Sala Cero
MAP N2 ■ Calle Sol 5 ■ 954 22 51 65 ■ www.salacero.com

This venue showcases regional music and theatre productions.

## 4 Teatro Alameda
C/Crédito 11 ■ 954 47 44 94 ■ www.teatroalamedasevilla.org

Contemporary Andalucían drama and flamenco feature strongly at this popular, modest theatre.

## 5 Teatro Central
MAP J1 ■ C/José de Gálvez 6, Isla de Cartuja ■ 955 54 21 55 ■ Closed Jul–Sep

In season, this theatre highlights the *Flamenco Viene del Sur* series, alongside all sorts of theatre, dance and classical music.

## 6 Tablao El Arenal
This venue has hosted flamenco performances for more than four decades. Visitors can enjoy tapas, drinks or a full meal while watching the performers. See the first show and the second is free.

## 7 La Carbonería
MAP N3 ■ C/Céspedes 21A ■ 954 22 99 45 ■ Shows Mon & Thu

A relaxed, authentic Flamenco bar with a good atmosphere.

## 8 Teatro Flamenco Sevilla
MAP M2 ■ C/Cuna 15 ■ Open 5:30pm, 7:30pm & 9pm daily ■ www.eatroflamencosevilla.com

A unique venue where acclaimed artists bring alive the emotions of flamenco, with dance and music.

## 9 Los Gallos
MAP N4 ■ Plaza de Santa Cruz 11 ■ 954 21 69 81 ■ Open 7pm & 8:45pm daily ■ www.tablaolosgallos.com

Excellent flamenco artists impress at the oldest *tablao* in Seville.

## 10 Teatro Lope de Vega
MAP M5 ■ Avda de María Luísa ■ 955 47 28 22 ■ www.teatrolopedevega.org

This Neo-Baroque theatre, named after the "Spanish Shakespeare", was built in 1929 as a casino and theatre for the Ibero-American Exposition. Modern and classical works are performed here.

**Stately interior of Lope de Vega theatre**

# Tapas Bars and Nightlife

**El Rinconcillo, arguably the most authentic tapas bar in Spain**

### 1 Sala Malandar
MAP K1 ▪ C/Torneo 43 ▪ 690 95 39 12 ▪ www.salamalandar.com

Come to this laid back club for an eclectic array of music – from funk to reggae and ska via soul, folk and indie pop – by live bands and DJs.

### 2 Premier Sherry Cocktail Bar
MAP L3 ▪ C/Jaén 1C ▪ 955 13 30 32

This vibrant bar offers an excellent selection of wine, sherry and cocktails. Tastings are available for groups.

### 3 Casa Morales
MAP L3 ▪ C/García de Vinuesa 11 ▪ 954 22 12 42

Reputedly the second-oldest bar in town (1850), and it doesn't seem to have changed much. Drinks are still poured from old casks. Simple tapas.

### 4 Antigüedades
MAP M3 ▪ C/Argote de Molina 40 ▪ 954 56 51 27

The eccentric decor of this bar, which changes regularly, features Roman and Arab elements. Traditional cuisine and reasonably priced drinks attract locals and tourists alike.

### 5 Pura Vida Terraza
MAP M3 ▪ Hotel Fontecruz, Calle Segovias 6 ▪ 667 71 74 44

At this lively rooftop pool and bar, you are invited to chill out, sip a cocktail and enjoy stunning views of the city. Beer and wine are also served.

### 6 El Rinconcillo
MAP M2 ▪ C/Gerona 40 ▪ 954 22 31 83

The city's oldest *taberna* dates from 1670 and is an essential stop on your Seville itinerary. Extensive choice of traditional Moorish-Andalucían food.

### 7 Antique Theatro
C/Matemáticos Rey Pastor y Castro, La Cartuja ▪ 666 55 05 50 ▪ Closed Mon–Wed

Dress to impress at Seville's most upscale club, and you might just get past the doormen. In summer, the terrace Rosso hosts live events.

### 8 La Terraza de EME
MAP M3 ▪ C/Alemanes 27, 4th Floor of EME Catedral Hotel ▪ 954 56 00 00

Enjoy the spectacular views of the cathedral and the Giralda while sipping a cocktail on the terrace bar of the upmarket Eme hotel.

### 9 Bar El Garlochi
MAP M2 ▪ C/Boteros 26 ▪ 666 66 66 66

A Seville institution with a religious decor. Expect Baroque exuberance and lively locals. Try the signature cocktail *Sangre de Cristo*.

### 10 Puratasca
MAP J3 ▪ C/Numancia 5 ▪ 954 33 16 21

Discover delicious twists on the classics at this fusion tapas bar, where the menu changes with the seasons.

# Places to Eat

**1 Restaurante Arte y Sabor**
MAP M1 ▪ Alameda de Hércules 85 ▪ 695 28 84 50 ▪ €

A selection of Moroccan and Spanish cuisine, with options for vegans and vegetarians, is offered at this restaurant. The terrace is a great place to sit back and enjoy the Alameda vibe.

**2 Lobo Lopez**
MAP L3 ▪ Calle de Rosario 15 ▪ 854 70 58 34 ▪ €

Tucked away on a side street, this smart restaurant offers a fusion of international cuisine. Try the scallop risotto with shrimp tartare.

**3 Casa La Viuda**
MAP L3 ▪ C/Albareda 2 ▪ 954 21 54 20 ▪ €

Choose from a wide variety of classic dishes and tapas at this Michelin-starred Sevillan bodega. Don't miss their famous cod.

Taberna del Alabardero

**4 Taberna del Alabardero**
MAP L3 ▪ C/Zaragoza 20 ▪ 954 50 27 21 ▪ €€

This superb restaurant has earned itself a Michelin star. The setting is sumptuous, while the menu excels in meat dishes and local seafood.

---

**PRICE CATEGORIES**
For a three-course meal for one with half a bottle of wine (or equivalent meal), taxes and extra charges
..................................................
€ under 30    €€ €30–€50    €€€ over 50

---

**5 El Disparate**
MAP M1 ▪ Alameda de Hercules 31 ▪ 680 12 74 13 ▪ €€

Expect fresh Mediterranean cuisine made using local and seasonal ingredients at this innovative Michelin-starred restaurant.

**6 Mechela Arenal**
MAP L3 ▪ C/Pastor y Landero 20 ▪ 955 28 25 66 ▪ €€

Mechela Arenal has a modern approach to traditional recipes using local ingredients. Try the white prawn carpaccio with avocado pesto.

**7 Casa Plácido**
MAP M3 ▪ C/Mesón del Moro 11 ▪ 954 56 39 71 ▪ €

A venerable bar offering hams dangling, barrels of sherry, old posters and traditional tapas.

**8 Abades Triana**
MAP L5 ▪ C/Betis 69 ▪ 954 28 64 59 ▪ €€€

This modern restaurant has a commanding location on the river. Diners can book a spot in El Cubo, a private area with a "floating" glass floor. There are tapas, tasting and gourmet tasting menus on offer.

**9 Espacio Eslava**
MAP L1 ▪ C/Eslava 3–5 ▪ 954 90 65 68 ▪ €€

This tapas bar and restaurant adds a dash of innovation to traditional cuisine using fresh, seasonal produce.

**10 Mariatrifulca**
MAP K4 ▪ Puente de Isabel II ▪ 954 33 03 47 ▪ €€

Enjoy a contemporary twist to classic Sevillian food while admiring stunning views of the city and the Guadalquivir.

*See map on p84*

# TOP 10 Sevilla and Huelva Provinces

Leaving behind the magnetic allure of glorious Seville, the rest of Sevilla Province and neighbouring Huelva Province are among the least visited areas of Andalucía. Much of the zone has remained a rural hinterland, where time moves slowly and the old customs prevail. Some of the finest nature preserves are here, too, including Parque Nacional de Doñana, mountainous reaches and pristine beaches, generally frequented by Spaniards rather than tourists. Culturally rich as well, each town and village shelters surprising art treasures and ancient marvels, where you may find yourself the only visitor – a welcome relief after the throngs encountered elsewhere in Andalucía.

**Bell tower, Écija**

## SEVILLA AND HUELVA PROVINCES

1 **Top 10 Sights**
see pp95–7

1 **Restaurants**
see p101

1 **Provincial Shopping**
see p99

1 **Cafés and Tapas Bars**
see p100

1 **The Best of the Rest**
see p98

**The Hermitage of El Rocío**

### 1 El Rocío
MAP B4

The fact that this town resembles an Old West frontier outpost is no accident. The Spaniards who settled what are now the states of Texas, New Mexico and Arizona mostly came from this part of Spain and took their architectural style with them. Horseback is still a normal way to get around here. The place bursts into life during the annual Romería (see p36), one of Spain's biggest festivals.

### 2 Parque Nacional de Doñana

Europe's largest nature reserve (see pp36–7) has important wetlands and shifting dunes that are gradually moving inland. The fragile area can only be visited on guided tours.

### 3 Huelva
MAP A4 ■ Museo de Huelva: Alameda Sundheim 13; 959 65 04 24; open Sep–Jun: 9am–9pm Tue–Sat, 9am–3pm Sun; adm (free to EU members)

Founded by the Phoenicians, Huelva was at its peak under the Romans – Huelva's provincial museum holds remarkable archaeological finds. The city's other claim to fame is as the starting point of Columbus's seafaring expedition. Huelva was the first port for Americas trade, before Seville took over.

**El Parque Minero de Ríotinto**

### 4 El Parque Minero de Ríotinto
MAP B3 ■ Museo Minero: Plaza Ernest Lluch; open 10:30am–3pm & 4–8pm Tue–Sun (Mon: until 7:30pm); adm ■ www.parquemineroderiotinto.es

The Ríotinto (Red River) mines, the world's oldest, have been exploited for minerals for some 5,000 years, and the gradual stripping away of the rich ore has left a weird moonscape shot through with coloured fissures. A museum details the mines' history.

**Carmona and its castle tower**

### ⑤ Carmona

**MAP C3** ■ Necrópolis: Avda Jorge Bonsor 9; 600 14 36 32; opening hours vary, call ahead for details; closed Mon

The closest major town east of Seville, Carmona has been continuously inhabited for more than 5,000 years. Its Roman remains are exceptional, especially the huge necropolis. The view from the originally Roman Puerta de Córdoba (Córdoba Gate) out over the sweeping plains shouldn't be missed. Fine churches, palaces and *alcázares* adorn the site – one of the ancient castles is now a spectacular parador *(see p141).*

### ⑥ Cazalla de la Sierra

**MAP C3** ■ La Cartuja de Cazalla arts centre; 951 19 34 46; open 11am–3pm Sat, Sun & public hols; adm; www.la cartujadecazalla.com

The main town in the Sierra Norte is a steep cluster of whitewashed houses. It's a popular place for weekend getaways by *sevillanos* and particularly known for produc-ing some of the area's famous anise-based tipples. Just 3 km (2 miles) outside of town is a former Carthusian monastery, restored as part hotel, part arts centre.

### ⑦ Écija

**MAP D3** ■ Museo Histórico Municipal: Palacio de Benamejí, C/Cánovas del Castillo 4; 955 90 29 19; opening hours vary, check website for details; closed Mon; museo.ecija.es

Two nicknames for this town east of Seville give an idea of its chief glory and its biggest challenge. "The Town of Towers" refers to its 11 Baroque bell towers, all adorned with glazed tiles. "The Frying-Pan of Andalucía" alludes to its searing summer temperatures, due to the fact that it's one of the few towns not on a hill. Écija's archaeological museum is worth a visit.

### ⑧ Osuna

**MAP D4** ■ Museo de Osuna: C/Sevilla 37; 954 81 57 32; open 10am–2pm & 5–8pm Tue–Sun (summer: 9:30am–2:30pm Tue–Thu, Sat & Sun, 9:30am–2:30pm & 7–9pm Fri)

**Exhibit in the Osuna museum**

The city of Osuna was an important hub of Renaissance Spain, which has resulted in some exceptional architecture such as the church, the Colegiata and the University. The Osuna Museum is home to, among a number of important artworks, a permanent exhibition dedicated to the popular TV series *Game of Thrones*, which was filmed here.

---

**SOCIALISM VERSUS FEUDALISM**

The fertile Campiña valley has been owned by a few noble families since the Catholic Monarchs handed out tracts as fiefdoms. The people who worked the land were little more than serfs, a situation that still accounts for local poverty. The mayor of Marinaleda, however, has created an island of social idealism, and has wrestled plots of property away from landlords to be communally owned by the workers.

### 9 Gruta de las Maravillas

MAP B3 ∎ C/Pozo de la Nieve, Aracena ∎ 663 93 78 76 ∎ Open 10am–1:30pm & 3–6pm daily ∎ Adm

A guided tour of these marvellous caves will wind through beautiful chambers with naturally coloured formations and names such as the Hut, Organ, Cathedral, Quail and Twins. The last room is a notorious crowd-pleaser – the *Sala de los Culos* (Chamber of the Buttocks). There are 12 caverns and six underground lakes. The "Great Lake" lies under a vaulted ceiling, 70 m (230 ft) high.

**Inside the Gruta de las Maravillas**

### 10 Itálica

MAP B3 ∎ Avda de Extremadura 2, Santiponce ∎ 600 141 767 ∎ Jan–mid-Jun & mid-Sep–Dec: 9am–6pm Tue–Sat, 9am–3pm Sun (mid-Mar–mid-Jun: open until 9pm Fri & Sat); mid-Jun–mid-Sep: 9am–3pm Tue–Sat ∎ Adm (free for EU members)

These wind-blown ruins were once the third-largest city in the Roman empire, founded in 206 BCE and home to half a million people during the reign of Emperor Hadrian in the 2nd century. He was following in the glorious footsteps of his predecessor Trajan, another Itálica native. There's an amphitheatre and some mosaics amid the crumbling walls. Most of the wonders are still buried, or have been moved to the Archaeological Museum in Seville (see p86).

## HALF A DAY IN SANTIPONCE

▶ **MORNING**

Venture 7 km (4 miles) north of Seville to Santiponce, a town famous for being the home of the ruins of the Roman city Itálica. Make your way to the **Monastery of San Isidoro del Campo** (*Avenida de San Isidoro del Campo 18*), founded in 1301 by Alonso Pérez de Guzmán. This vast complex is home to two churches, and is a juxtaposition of Gothic, Baroque, Languedoc and Mudejar design.

From the monastery, take a 20 minute walk north to the **Cotidiana Vitae** (*Plaza de la Constitución*), close to the **Teatro Romano de Italica** (*currently open only for concerts or plays*). This cultural centre recreates the daily life of the Romans of the 2nd century, both in their homes and in the street.

Leaving the centre, head north on Avenida de Extremadura and turn right on Avda Rocio Vega to reach **La Caseta De Antonio** (*Avda Rocío Vega 10; 955 99 63 06*) for lunch. Try one of the delectable rice dishes here.

**AFTERNOON**

After lunch, head to **Itálica**, the first Roman city on the Iberian peninsula. Stroll through the grounds of the ancient settlement, passing some astonishing mosaics, a temple, the remains of thermal baths and the 2,500-seat amphitheatre.

Round off the afternoon with a cup of coffee from your pick of one of the Spanish restaurants near the ruins.

*See map on pp94–5* ←

# The Best of the Rest

### ① Jabugo
MAP B3

The "home of ham" produces Spain's most famous, known as *jamón ibérico* (cured Iberian ham), *jamón serrano* (mountain-cured ham) and *pata negra*, named after the black pigs that forage in the Sierra de Aracena.

### ② Niebla
MAP B4

Massive ramparts, built by the Moors in the 12th century, attest to the central role this town played in defending the land. The walls stretch for about 2.5 km (1.5 miles).

### ③ Sierra de Aracena y Picos de Aroche Park
MAP B2

This wild area *(see p60)* provides plenty of inspiring views and fauna.

### ④ Aroche
MAP A2 ■ Museo del Santo Rosario: Calle Fray Juan Bross ■ 859 99 30 38 ■ Open mid-May–Sep: 11am–3pm Thu–Sun & public hols; Oct–mid-May: 10am–2pm & 4–6pm Fri–Sun & public hols

This well-preserved village contains a wonderful oddity, the Museo del Santo Rosario, packed with rosaries that have belonged to Mother Teresa, John F Kennedy and General Franco.

### ⑤ Cortegana
MAP B3

A 13th-century castle dominates one of the largest towns in the area.

**The town of Cortegana**

### ⑥ Aracena
MAP B3

Capital of the sierra, this is a lovely little town. The crumbling castle offers views of the surrounding hills.

### ⑦ Almonaster la Real
MAP B3

A 10th-century mosque *(see p44)* and castle, as well as a bullring, are clustered on a citadel overlooking the village *(see p56)*.

**The Mezquita at Almonaster la Real**

### ⑧ Santa Olalla del Cala
MAP B3

In the heart of the ham-curing area, this village has a 13th-century castle and a 15th-century Baroque church.

### ⑨ Alájar
MAP B3

A small town *(see p56)* of cobbled streets and white-washed buildings.

### ⑩ Zufre
MAP B3

This cliff-top community is like a mini-Ronda *(see pp30–31)*. The Paseo de los Alcaldes has rose and lime trees and views across the plain.

# Provincial Shopping

**1 Aroche Markets**
Thursday is the day the market stalls arrive in this Huelvan town. The market in Plaza de Abastos features a traditional produce spread, including the strong-flavoured goat's cheese favoured by the locals.

**2 Souvenirs**
In Aracena, head for the Calle Pozo de la Nieve, a cobbled street lined with souvenir shops. In El Rocío *(see p95)*, souvenir stalls flank the church, hawking paraphernalia associated with the famous Romería pilgrimage *(see p36)*.

**3 Crafts**
In addition to leather, Valverde del Camino is known for furniture and fine wooden boxes. Embroidery work from Aracena and Bollullos del Condado is worth seeking out, as well as linen tablecloths from Cortegana and Moguer. Wickerwork is widely sold around Huelva, while nearer the coast it is also common to see Moroccan goods for sale.

**4 Pottery**
In this area, pottery has traditional patterns influenced by Moorish art. Look for water jugs, plates and jars, decorated in blue, green and white glazes.

**5 Leather**
The most notable leather goods come from Valverde del Camino. Choose *botos camperos* (cowboy boots) or the longer *botos rocieros* (Spanish riding boots). Many shops produce footwear, and a number of crafters make boots to order, taking three to four days to make a pair. There are workshops devoted to making saddles and bridles.

*Jamón ibérico* **from Jabugo**

**6 Ham**
The Mesón Sánchez Romero Carvajal in Jabugo is one of the top producers of the local *jamón ibérico*.

**7 El Condado Wine District**
The name refers to an area noted for its reliable white wine. Local *finos* include Condado Pálido and Condado Viejo.

**8 Anise Liqueur**
The liqueur of choice throughout the region is anise-based. One of the best is Anis Cazalla from the eponymous town *(see p96)*.

**Local pottery**

**9 Huelva**
The provincial capital *(see p95)* has its own El Corte Inglés department store on Plaza de España, while the area around it and just off Plaza 12 de Octobre constitutes the main shopping district. The Mercadillo (open-air market) is held every Friday on the Recinto Colombino.

**10 Cured Fish**
Considered a great delicacy and priced accordingly, raw wind-cured tuna *(mojama)* is an acquired taste. Isla Cristina is the main centre of production, but you can buy it in the Mercado del Carmen in Huelva, and other food markets.

*See map on pp94–5*

# Cafés and Tapas Bars

An appetizing tapas platter

### (1) Bar Plus Ultra, La Rábida

MAP A4 ▪ Avenida de America 34 ▪ 959 53 00 34 ▪ Closed Mon

Close to the Monasterio de Santa María de la Rábida, this traditional, family-friendly restaurant serves fabulous tapas.

### (2) Bar Goya, Carmona

MAP C3 ▪ C/Prim 2 ▪ 954 14 30 60 ▪ Closed Wed

This restaurant is set in a 15th-century, Moorish-style building in the heart of Carmona. Andalucían home cooking with a modern twist is the speciality here.

### (3) El Martinete, Cazalla

MAP C3 ▪ Ctra Estación de Cazalla km 12 ▪ 687 49 39 65 (information) ▪ Closed Mon–Wed

Enjoy good-value tapas and seasonal, local produce in a beautiful setting sorrounded by woods and waterfalls.

### (4) Bar La Reja, Écija

MAP D3 ▪ C/Cintería 16 ▪ 954 83 30 12 ▪ Closed Sun & Mon

This local favourite offers a wide choice of tapas and raciones and the leisurely atmosphere invites lingering.

### (5) La Puerta Ancha, Ayamonte

MAP A4 ▪ Plaza de la Laguna 14 ▪ 686 44 74 64 ▪ Closed Sun

A sociable place that purports to be the original town bar. There are tables on the square and good prices, too, for their line of drinks, tapas and other snacks.

### (6) Espuma del Mar, Isla Canela

MAP A4 ▪ Paseo de los Gavilanes 28 ▪ 959 47 72 85

This beachside establishment has alfresco tables and tasty tapas. The speciality is, of course, fresh fish and seafood. Try raya (skate) in one of its various manifestations.

### (7) El Refugio, Mazagón

MAP B4 ▪ C/Santa Clara 43 ▪ 624 52 69 79 ▪ Closed Tue

A laid-back, popular haunt in this surfer's paradise. Located a short stroll from the beach, El Refugio is renowned for its fresh fish dishes.

### (8) Mesón La Reja, Aracena

MAP B3 ▪ Ctra N433 km 87 ▪ 959 12 76 70

This tapas bar specializes in regional food including wild mushrooms, local cheeses and snails.

### (9) Café Bar Manzano, Aracena

MAP B3 ▪ Plaza del Marqués de Aracena 22 ▪ 672 60 54 56 ▪ Closed Wed

On the south side of the town square this traditional bar is a classic Sierra place for coffee and a pastry.

### (10) Casa Curro, Osuna

MAP D4 ▪ Plazuela Salitre 5 ▪ 955 82 07 58 ▪ Closed Mon

A few blocks from the main square, this is a premier tapas bar. Worth seeking out for the quality.

Patatas bravas

# Restaurants

### 1 La Choza de Manuela, Bormujos
MAP B4 ▪ C/Menendez Pidal 2 ▪ 649 44 56 16 ▪ €

Popular with locals, this restaurant specializes in a variety of succulent, grilled meats, served by friendly staff. Go early to avoid the long queues.

### 2 Meson Rey Arturo, Osuna
MAP D4 ▪ C/Sor Angela 3 ▪ 662 13 22 21 ▪ Closed Sun–Tue; Sat D ▪ €€

Feast on creative interpretations of regional and international cuisine, such as *croquetas de chipirones en su tinta con alioli de higo* (squid croquettes in their ink with fig alioli).

### 3 Restaurante Miramar, Punta Umbría
MAP A4 ▪ C/Miramar 1 ▪ 959 31 12 43 ▪ €

Fresh fish from the Atlantic is paired with rice dishes.

### 4 Restaurante Montecruz, Aracena
MAP B3 ▪ Plaza de San Pedro 36 ▪ 959 12 60 13 ▪ €€

Local, organic produce is key, with game, ham, chestnuts and wild mushrooms when in season. Exceptional food in both the restaurant and tapas bar.

### 5 Cambio de Tercio, Constantina
MAP C3 ▪ C/Virgen del Robledo 53 bajo, Constantina ▪ 955 88 10 80 ▪ Closed Tue & Sun–Thu D ▪ €

This place is popular with devotees of rural cookery. Specialities include Iberian pork loin in wild mushroom sauce and for dessert *tarta de castañas* (chestnut tart).

### 6 Restaurante Azabache, Huelva
MAP A4 ▪ C/Vázquez López 22 ▪ 959 25 75 28 ▪ Closed Sat D, Sun ▪ €€€

A smart traditional restaurant that's popular with locals (later in the evening) and is known for its *raciones*, or large servings of tapas.

### 7 Casa Luciano, Ayamonte
MAP A4 ▪ C/Palma del Condado 1 ▪ 959 47 10 71 ▪ Closed Sun D, Mon ▪ €€

The place for fresh, tempting seafood and fish stews. Try the delicious *coquinas* (steamed baby clams) or the appetizing grilled calamari.

*Choza*-style façade of Aires de Doñana

### 8 Aires de Doñana, El Rocío
MAP B4 ▪ Avda La Canaliega 1 ▪ 959 44 22 89 ▪ Closed Sun D, Mon, 20 days in Jul ▪ €€

French windows provide panoramic views of the marshes here. Sample the goose liver pâté, beef burger and the blueberry cheesecake.

### 9 Posada de Cortegana, Cortegana
MAP A2 ▪ Ctra El Repilado – La Corte km 2.5 ▪ 959 50 33 17 ▪ €€

A wide variety of meat, such as Iberian pork, venison and game, is on offer at this lovely grillhouse.

### 10 Casa El Padrino, Alájar
MAP B3 ▪ Plaza Miguel Moya 2 ▪ 959 12 56 01 ▪ Closed Sun D & Mon–Thu ▪ €

This rustic favourite is known for its tasty regional cuisine.

*See map on pp94–5* ←

# TOP 10 Málaga and Cádiz Provinces

These two Andalucían provinces are a heady mix of cultural and recreational riches. Europe's oldest city, Cádiz, is found here, but the presence of history is balanced by the hedonistic delights of the Costa del Sol and its fine beaches. Some of the region's most dramatic landscapes lure nature-lovers, while others are drawn by the charms of the famed *pueblos blancos* (white villages), the most renowned being Ronda, birthplace of that strongest of Spanish traditions, the bullfight. This is also the area that produces the world-famous fortified wines known as *Jerez* (sherry), as well as the celebrated sweet wines of Málaga. Finally, Europe's southernmost point is located here, Tarifa, with views of North Africa, and a stone's throw away, the Rock of Gibraltar.

**A tower of Catedral Nueva in Cádiz**

## MÁLAGA AND CÁDIZ PROVINCES

**Puento Nuevo, Ronda**

### 1 Ronda

To many visitors over the centuries, this town evokes the "real" Andalucía, wild and spectacular. This mountain rock eyrie is breathtaking, being dramatically sliced down the middle by El Tajo, a fantastically deep and narrow limestone ravine, formed over thousands of years by the Río Guadalevín. Thus Ronda is a town of two halves – the ancient half is steeped in rich Moorish history, with cobbled streets, while the more modern part is on the north side (see pp30–31).

### 2 Cádiz

At the apex of the Atlantic's untamed Costa de la Luz (see p106), ancient Cádiz floats on what was originally its own island. It is possibly Europe's oldest city, thought to have been founded by the Phoenicians in around 1104 BCE. Much of what can be seen today, however, dates from the 18th century – the city was destroyed by an Anglo-Dutch raid in 1596. Catedral Nueva (1722) is one of Spain's largest churches, and many Baroque edifices enhance this unpretentiously beautiful provincial capital. Apart from two weeks in February when Cádiz stages Spain's most celebrated Carnaval (see p80), it remains under-visited (see pp26–7).

**Roman amphitheatre, Málaga**

### 3 Málaga

MAP E5 ▪ Museo Picasso:
C/San Agustín 8 ▪ 952 12 76 00
▪ Open 10am–7pm daily ▪ Adm
▪ www.museopicassomalaga.org

Despite being home to the main airport bringing holidaymakers to the Costa del Sol, this provincial capital has been bypassed by the brunt of "sun coast" development and has managed to hold onto its Spanish-ness quite admirably. It has a thriving arts scene and attracts foodies to its many restaurants. The modern waterfront complex has bars, shops, the Centre Pompidou Málaga museum (see p52), a promenade and space for plush yachts. Important as a trading port since ancient times, it was the favourite city of poet García Lorca (see p55), who loved its rawness. But its even greater claim to artistic fame is that it was the birthplace of Pablo Picasso, whose creative genius is celebrated in the Picasso museum (see p52). Málaga's alcázar, built between the 8th and 11th centuries, includes a Roman amphitheatre.

### 4 Antequera

MAP D4 ▪ Museo Municipal:
Palacio Nájera, Plaza del Coso Viejo
▪ 952 70 83 00 ▪ Open Tue–Sun ▪ Adm

So ancient that even the Romans called it Antiquaria, this market town presents a wonderfully condensed architectural history of the entire area, beginning with Neolithic dolmens dating from between 4500 and 2500 BCE. In addition, there are significant Roman ruins, including villas with outstanding mosaics, a Moorish Alcazaba, the 16th-century Arco de los Gigantes and fine Renaissance palaces and churches to explore. Many treasures originally found in the town – including the exquisite Ephebe of Antequera, a rare, life-size Roman bronze statue of a young boy – are displayed in the Municipal Museum, housed in an 18th-century palace.

### 5 Gibraltar

MAP C6

This gargantuan chunk of limestone rising up from the Mediterranean was one of the mythic Pillars of Hercules. Yet, despite being nicknamed "The Rock", as a worldwide symbol of stability and security, this fortress is the subject of contention between Spain and Great Britain.

**The Rock of Gibraltar**

Nonetheless, many people cross the border to visit this slice of England today. The town centre is home to museums, restaurants and shops, and from here visitors can take a cable car to the Upper Rock. Here, several interesting attractions can be found, including St. Michael's Cave, the tunnels from the Great Siege of 1779–83 and tunnels from World War II. The Skywalk lookout, perched at 340 m (1,115 ft) above sea level, and the Windsor Suspension Bridge offer incredible views. Don't miss the Apes' Den, which houses one of Gibraltar's most iconic residents: the Barbary Macaques (tailless monkeys).

**Casares, a pretty *pueblo blanco***

### 6 Pueblos Blancos
MAP C5

The term "white villages" refers to the profusion of whitewashed hillside hamlets in the Serranía de Ronda, the mountainous territory around Ronda. Many are truly beautiful and it's well worth spending several days driving from one to the other, and then striking out on foot to take in some of the views *(see p69)*. Towns not to miss include Gaucín, Casares, Grazalema, Setenil, Zahara de la Sierra *(see p57)*, Jimena de Libár and Manilva. Villagers, who originally settled here to protect themselves from bandits in the lowlands, retain a centuries-old way of life and strong agricultural tradition. Between Grazalema and Zahara, you'll go through Andalucía's highest mountain pass, the breathtaking Puerto de las Palomas (The Pass of the Doves).

---

### A MORNING WALK IN JEREZ DE LA FRONTERA

▶ **MORNING**

Begin your tour at the impressive Alcázar, with its many Moorish remains, including restored gardens, a mosque and a *hammam* (baths), and a *camera obscura* providing views of the city and beyond. Beside it is the stunningly decorated cathedral, extravagantly rich inside and out. Note the fine painting of *The Sleeping Girl* by Zurbarán in the sacristy.

Next take the tour – with tastings – of the **González-Byass bodega** *(see p76)*, possibly the oldest cellars in Jerez, including one designed by Gustave Eiffel. Don't miss the many signatures of famous people on the barrels (called "butts"), including Queen Victoria, Cole Porter, Martin Luther King and General Franco, among others.

Continuing on north, the **Bodegas Fundador** *(see p76)* also offers tours and is distinctively Moorish in style. A block further north, pass the Gothic style Church of San Mateo, then pop into the **Museo Arqueológico** to see the prized Greek bronze helmet from the 7th century BCE, and then enter the **Barrio de Santiago**. This gently dilapidated neighbourhood of maze-like alleyways is home to a sizeable Roma community and numerous flamenco venues.

To cap off your walk, continue southeast out of the *barrio*, past the **Church of San Dionisio**, then turn back to **Tabanco Plateros** *(C/Algarve 35; 956 10 44 58)*, for some light tapas and a great selection of wine and cheese.

*See map on pp102–3*

### 7 Arcos de la Frontera

MAP C5 ■ Galería de Arte Arx-Arcis: C/Marqués de Torresoto 11 ■ 956 70 39 51 ■ Open 10:30am–8:30pm daily

Another town built atop a sheer cliff, this is probably the most dazzling of the *pueblos blancos* and the one situated furthest west. Little remains of the period before the *reconquista*, when it received its "de la Frontera" appellation, as a bastion "on the frontier" between Christian and Moorish Spain. The Galería de Arte Arx-Arcis crafts museum and shop displays local carpets, blankets, baskets and pottery.

### 8 The Costa del Sol

This string of former Mediterranean fishing villages still lives up to its reputation as one of the world centres for sun, surf and fun. But beyond the bustling tourist enclaves there is still much authentic charm on offer and even places that invite tranquility – especially in the towns of Estepona, Nerja, Mijas and ultra-classy Marbella *(see p65)*. Year-round golf makes the whole area a great attraction for international fans of the sport *(see p109)* and, in high

**Nerja beach, The Costa del Sol**

season in particular, Torremolinos *(see p33)* is the place to find some of Spain's liveliest nightlife.

### 9 Jerez de la Frontera

MAP B5 ■ Alcázar de Jerez: C/Alameda Vieja ■ 650 80 01 00 ■ Open Jul–Sep: 9:30am–6pm; Oct–Jun: 9:30am–3pm daily; seasonal hours vary, call ahead to check ■ Adm

The largest city in Cádiz Province is synonymous with "sherry", which is a corruption of "Jerez" – itself a corruption of the Phoenician name of Xeres *(see pp76–7)*. Before that, it was part of the fabled Tartessian civilization (8th century BC). Sights include Jerez's Moorish fortress, once part of a 4-km (2.5-mile) wall *(see p105)*. A well-preserved mosque, now the Santa María La Real chapel, features an octagonal cupola over the *mihrab* (prayer niche). Jerez is renowned for equestrian art, Andalucían style, as well as for flamenco *(see pp50–51)*.

### 10 The Costa de la Luz

MAP B5–C6

Named for its shimmering sunlight *(luz)*, the stretch of coast from Huelva down to Tarifa is opposite to the Costa del Sol; its low-key resorts attract mainly Spanish visitors and watersports lovers – the latter drawn by the strong ocean breezes. But there are plenty of pretty beaches, many backed by shady pine forests, and the combination of Arabic forts, Moorish castles, medieval churches, sherry and old-school charm makes the Costa de la Luz a great choice for adventurous holidaymakers.

---

**THE SHERRY TRIANGLE**

Jerez, Sanlúcar de Barrameda and El Puerto de Santa María mark the famed "Sherry Triangle". Production of the fortified wine (**above**) was started by the Phoenicians using vines they imported some 3,000 years ago. In Roman times it was exported all over the empire, and it has been popular in England since the Elizabethan age. Sherry varies in degrees of dryness or sweetness. The *fino* and *manzanilla* are dry and light, while the *amontillado* and *oloroso* are more robust *(see p77)*.

# The Best of the Rest

### 1 El Torcal de Antequera
MAP D4

This mountain nature reserve (see p60) is great for hiking. The odd limestone rock formations are a big draw.

### 2 El Chorro
MAP D4

A geographical wonder, the Chorro Gorge's immense chasm, 180-m (590-ft) high, was created by the Río Guadalorce slashing through the limestone mountain. A 7.7-km- (4.7-mile-) long path, the El Caminito del Rey, runs along the gorge.

El Caminito del Rey

### 3 Grazalema
MAP C5

Nestled in the foothills of the Sierra del Pinar, Grazalema is a charming village – Spain's rainiest, according to some – and the main access point for the Sierra de Grazalema Natural Park, one of the best hiking areas in Andalucía (see p60). Known for its local cheeses, stews and honey, it's also a great place to plan a picnic.

### 4 Tarifa
MAP C6

One of Andalucía's hippest coastal towns (see p64), Tarifa features a sizable windsurfing and kitesurfing (see p66) contingent and various Moroccan touches.

### 5 Algeciras
MAP C6

Although the town of Algeciras is industrial and polluted, its port is the best in Spain; from here you can catch the ferry to Morocco. Peruse the Moorish bazaars while waiting for the boat to take you across.

### 6 El Puerto de Santa María
MAP B5

One of the Sherry Triangle towns, several bodegas (see p76) can be visited here for tours and tastings.

### 7 Sanlúcar de Barrameda
MAP B5

Famed for its manzanilla sherry and superb seafood, the town also offers beautiful churches, palaces and tours of the bodegas.

### 8 Chipiona
MAP B5

This pretty resort town is crowded with Spanish beach enthusiasts in high season. The pace of life here is leisurely, consisting of enjoying the surf and miles of golden sand during the day, then strolls and ice cream until late in the evening.

### 9 Vejer de la Frontera
MAP C6

Of all the pueblos blancos (see p105), this one has kept its Moorish roots most intact. Its original four Moorish gates still stand and its streets have barely changed in 1,000 years.

### 10 Medina Sidonia
MAP C5 ■ Iglesia de Santa María la Coronada: Plaza Iglesia Mayor; 956 41 03 29; opening hours vary, call ahead for details; adm

The most important edifice here is the 15th-century church of Santa María la Coronada, built over an earlier mosque. The interior features a 15-m (50-ft) high retablo.

See map on pp102–3 ⬅

# Provincial Shopping

### 1 Málaga Wines
MAP Q5 ▪ El Templo del Vino: C/de Sebastián Souvirón 11, Málaga ▪ 952 21 75 03

The region is famed for its sweet wines (see p77), and Málaga has plenty of establishments where they can be sampled and purchased. El Templo del Vino is particularly well stocked with local tipples and also with wines from all over Spain.

**Delicacies in a Málaga grocer**

### 2 Chocolates Artesanales Frigiliana
MAP E5 ▪ C/Real 27, Frigiliana ▪ 669 20 90 56

Set in a picturesque village, Chocolates Artesanales Frigiliana sells over 15 unique chocolate flavours and a range of cosmetics, all made with a natural chocolate base.

### 3 Deligades, Cádiz
MAP B5 ▪ C/Libertad 9 ▪ 956 21 35 21

This gourmet shop sells an array of wine, cheese, ham, olive oil, sweets and other delicacies of the region.

### 4 Xauen, Conil de la Frontera
MAP B5 ▪ C/Cádiz 33 ▪ 661 27 14 30

A specialist in expertly crafted leather goods, this shop offers wallets, bags and bracelets.

### 5 Flamenco Costumes
MAP B5 ▪ Tamara Flamenco: C/Santa Maria 5, Jerez ▪ 956 34 74 89

Jerez is one of the very best places to find genuine flamenco gear.

### 6 Equestrian Equipment
MAP B5 ▪ Hipisur: C/Circo 1, Jerez ▪ 956 32 42 09 ▪ www.hipi sur.com

Jerez has to be one of the best places in the world to find refined horse-riding gear. Hipisur has an extensive range of clothing and kit.

### 7 Sherry
Jerez de la Frontera is, of course, also the prime spot to savour the finer points of a *fino*, a *manzanilla*, an *amontillado* or an *oloroso*. Tasting tours are available at most *bodegas* (see pp76–7).

### 8 Traditional Textiles
The villages of Grazalema and Arcos de la Frontera (see p106) are known for their blankets, ponchos, rugs and other woven textiles.

### 9 Shopping in Gibraltar
MAP C6

The shopping draw here is twofold: there's no sales tax and it's mostly duty-free. Several UK high-street names are represented, such as Next and Marks & Spencer.

### 10 Leather
In the shops of Ronda (see pp30–31) you'll find some of the best prices on leather goods of anywhere in Spain. Many of the items have well-known labels, since fashion houses often have contracts with leather factories in this area.

**Shopping in Ronda**

# Costa del Sol Golf Courses

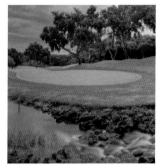

**Lush greens on the Valderrama course**

### 1 Valderrama
MAP C6 ■ Avda los Cortijos s/n San Roque ■ 956 79 12 00 ■ www.valderrama.com

The most famous golf club along the Costa, the Valderrama has hosted the Ryder Cup and is a Robert Trent Jones masterpiece.

### 2 Real Club de Golf Sotogrande
MAP D6 ■ Paseo del Parque, Sotogrande ■ 956 78 50 14 ■ www.golfsotogrande.com

Royal Sotogrande opened in 1964 and remains one of Europe's top 10 courses. Green-fee-paying visitors are welcome if they book in advance. The Robert Trent Jones design features mature trees and water obstacles.

### 3 San Roque
MAP C6 ■ N340 km 126.5, San Roque ■ 956 61 30 30 ■ www.sanroqueclub.com

San Roque offers two courses: one with holes that are in the direction of the prevailing wind, and another with a variety of challenges.

### 4 Real Club Las Brisas
MAP D5 ■ Urbanización Nueva Calle Londres 1 (Andalucía), above Puerto Banús, Marbella ■ 952 81 08 75 ■ www.realclubdegolflasbrisas.com

Recognized as one of the finest courses in Europe, this was also designed by Robert Trent Jones. The grounds have raised greens, sand traps and water features. It has hosted the World Cup twice and the Spanish Open three times.

### 5 La Hacienda Alcaidesa Links
MAP C6 ■ Avda del Golf, San Roque ■ 956 79 10 40 ■ www.lahaciendagolf.com

The only links course in Spain, Alcaidesa opened in 1992 and has been redesigned.

### 6 Golf El Paraíso
MAP D5 ■ Ctra de Cádiz km 167, Estepona ■ 952 88 38 35 ■ www.elparaisogolf.com

This British-style golf venue was designed by Gary Player.

### 7 Los Arqueros
MAP D5 ■ Ctra de Ronda A397 km 44.5, Benahavis ■ 952 78 46 00 ■ www.losarquerosgolf.com

The Costa's first course to be designed by Seve Ballesteros is a tough test.

### 8 Miraflores
MAP D5 ■ Urbanización Riviera del Sol, Ctra de Cádiz km 198, Calle Severiano Ballesteros ■ 952 93 19 60 ■ www.miraflores-golf.com

Folco Nardi's design has many challenging holes.

### 9 La Duquesa
MAP D5 ■ Urbanización El Hacho, N340 km 143, Manilva ■ 952 89 07 25 ■ www.golfladuquesa.com

A Trent Jones design, the front nine holes begin in a westerly direction then finish with a long par five.

### 10 La Cañada
MAP C6 ■ Ctra Guadiaro km 1, Guadiaro, San Roque ■ 956 79 41 00 ■ www.lacanadagolf.com

The long 1st hole sets the tone for a tough round – the 4th offers no view of the green until the third shot.

*See map on pp102–3*

# Costa del Sol Nightlife

### ① Ocean Club, Marbella
MAP D5 ■ Avda Lola Flores
■ 952 90 81 37 ■ www.oceanclub.es
A chic club featuring a saltwater swimming pool and a VIP area with huge round beds.

### ② La Suite, Marbella
MAP D5 ■ Puente Romano Hotel, Bulevar Príncipe Alfonso von Hohenlohe, Ctra de Cádiz km 177
■ 952 89 09 00 ■ Closed Sun–Wed
Live it up at this club with fire-eaters, belly dancers and jugglers. In the summer, the club becomes Suite del Mar and moves beachside.

### ③ Club de Jazz y Cócteles Speakeasy, Fuengirola
MAP D5 ■ C/María Barranco 1, 29640 Fuengirola ■ 656 48 79 19
Styled after the speakeasies of the 1920s, this bar has live jazz music at weekends and great cocktails.

### ④ El Mico Bar, Torremolinos
MAP D5 ■ Edificio Delphine, C. Jaén, 2, Local 13 ■ 711 01 17 15
Karaoke, quiz nights, drag shows and live entertainment are offered at this bar.

### ⑤ Olivia Valère, Marbella
MAP D5 ■ Ctra de Istán km 0.8
■ 952 82 88 61 ■ www.oliviavalere. com
This exclusive club is a Costa hot spot. Designed by the same creative genius who did Paris's famous Buddha Bar, it attracts a well-heeled crowd.

**Diners at Olivia Valère**

### ⑥ Puerto Marina, Benalmádena
MAP D5 ■ Puerto Marina
A large complex with a variety of bars, nightclubs, shops and restaurants.

### ⑦ Mango, Benalmádena
MAP D5 ■ Plaza Solymar
■ 952 56 27 00
Popular with the younger crowds, this club has an electric atmosphere.

**Dancing crowds at Mango**

### ⑧ Gran Madrid Casino Torrequebrada, Benalmádena
MAP D5 ■ Avda del Sol ■ 952 57 73 00
■ www.casinotorrequebrada.com
Located in the Hotel Torrequebrada, the casino has tables for blackjack, chemin de fer, punto y banco and roulette. Dress smart.

### ⑨ La Taberna de Pepe Lopez, Torremolinos
MAP E5 ■ Plaza de la Gamba Alegre
■ 952 38 12 84 ■ Closed Sun
This flamenco venue is highly touristy, but fun. Shows take place here between 10pm and midnight.

### ⑩ Torremolinos for LGBTQ+ Nightlife
MAP E5
Torremolinos has the best LGBTQ+ nightlife on the Costa del Sol. Start at terrace bar El Gato (Paseo Marítimo Antonio Machado 1), then try Parthenon (Calle Nogalera). Centuryon (Calle Casablanca 15) is the biggest LGBTQ+ club outside Madrid or Barcelona.

# Costa del Sol Places to Eat

**PRICE CATEGORIES**
For a three-course meal for one with half a bottle of wine (or equivalent meal), taxes and extra charges.

€ under €30  €€ €30–€50  €€€ over €50

## 1 La Pappardella, Marbella

MAP D5 ▪ Muelle de Honor, Casa A, local 4, Puerto Banus ▪ 952 81 50 89 ▪ €€€

Enjoy true Neapolitan cuisine at this family-orientated restaurant with a wide range of pasta, pizza and seafood.

## 2 El Tintero II, Málaga

MAP E5 ▪ Avda Salvador Allende 340 ▪ 650 68 09 56 ▪ €

This open-air fish restaurant on the beach offers a wide range of fresh seafood.

## 3 El Estrecho, Marbella

MAP D5 ▪ C/San Lázaro 12 ▪ 609 40 93 36 ▪ Closed Sun ▪ €

Another winning tapas bar and local favourite. There's a terrace, seafood treats and nice *fino*. Try the *boquerones al limón* (anchovies in lemon).

## 4 La Sirena, Benalmádena

MAP D5 ▪ Paseo Maritimo ▪ 951 08 07 12 ▪ Closed Mon ▪ €€

On the beachfront, and the paella is one of the best in the area.

## 5 Bodegas Quitapenas, Torremolinos

MAP E5 ▪ C/Cuesta del Tajo 3 ▪ 952 38 62 44 ▪ €

An excellent tapas bar with Spanish seafood, including *pulpo* (octopus).

## 6 Restaurante La Experiencia, Torremolinos

MAP E5 ▪ Avda Joan Miró 19, L6 Entrada ▪ 623 43 08 63 ▪ Closed L, Sun & Mon ▪ €€€

This intimate and cosy restaurant promises an indulgent fine dining experience.

## 7 Tapeo de Cervantes, Malaga

MAP E5 ▪ C/Cárcer 8 ▪ 952 60 94 58 ▪ Closed Mon ▪ www.eltapeo decervantes.com ▪ €€

This charming, rustic *bodega* serves hearty regional food with some novel touches. Try the *estofado de cordero* (lamb stew with mint and couscous).

## 8 Bar Altamirano, Marbella

MAP D5 ▪ Plaza Altamirano 3 ▪ 952 82 49 32 ▪ Closed Wed ▪ €

Despite Marbella's glitzy image there are affordable, traditional tapas bars. This is one of them, just southeast of Plaza Naranjos; seafood specialities are listed on ceramic menus.

Alfresco dining at Bar Altamirano

## 9 Restaurante 34, Nerja

MAP E5 ▪ C/Hernando de Carabeo 34 ▪ 952 52 54 44 ▪ €€€

Cut into the cliff, the café gives views of the sea while you are protected under palm frond umbrellas.

## 10 Lan Sang, Nerja

MAP E5 ▪ C/Malaga 12 ▪ 952 52 80 53 ▪ Closed Sun & Mon L ▪ €€

For a change of cuisine, try this Thai/Laotian restaurant. The modern, elegant decor is matched by the sophisticated flavours and beautiful presentation of the food.

*See map on pp102–3*

# Nightlife in the Region

An evening out in Nerja

### 1 Nerja by Night
MAP E5 ▪ Pub New Seven: Plaza Tutti Frutti ▪ Sala Rockerfeller: C/Chaparil 7

If you're looking for nightlife in Nerja, head to Plaza Tutti Frutti where there are around 25 bars and nightspots offering everything from cocktails to karaoke. Two of the best-known clubs here are Seven and the nearby Sala Rockerfeller.

### 2 Barsovia, Málaga
MAP R4 ▪ C/Mendez Nuñez 3

This old-town disco attracts people of all ages. The music is a mix of 1980s feel-good, with some current hits thrown in.

### 3 ZZ Pub, Málaga
MAP Q4 ▪ C/Tejón y Rodríguez 6

Mostly students come to this modest establishment in the old town to hear the bands that play here on weekdays. A DJ fills in the quiet moments every night.

### 4 Tarifa
MAP C6 ▪ Almedina Tarifa: C/Almedina 3 ▪ Café del Mar: Paseo Marítimo

Almedina Tarifa is one of the oldest and most beautiful bars in town, with flamenco on Thursday nights. Nightclub Café del Mar has three floors including a roof terrace.

### 5 Cádiz
MAP B5 ▪ Momart Theatre: Paseo Pascual Pery Junquera ▪ 660 58 04 86 ▪ Open Fri & Sat ▪ Adm

The zone around the harbour is loaded with venues and Momart Theatre is one of the best.

### 6 Flamenco in Cádiz
MAP B5 ▪ Peña La Perla: C/Concepción Arenal 0 ▪ Peña Enrique el Mellizo: Punta San Felipe, C/Nuevo Mundo 1

The flamenco clubs burst with life in Cádiz. Good bets include Peña La Perla and Peña Enrique el Mellizo.

### 7 Flamenco in Jerez
MAP B5

Here you will find genuine flamenco at its impassioned best. The Roma quarter of Santiago is the place to make for, where you will find a number of peñas (clubs), but don't expect much before 10pm.

### 8 Ronda
MAP D5 ▪ Café Las Bridas: C/Virgen de los Remedios 18 ▪ Café Pub Dulcinea: C/Rios Rosas 3

Café Las Bridas offers imported brews, with live music on weekends from midnight. Dance to Spanish electro-pop at Café Pub Dulcinea.

### 9 Gibraltar
MAP C6

There are more than 360 pubs in Gibraltar. If you enjoy late nights you should visit Queensway Quay, Marina Bay and Casemates Square, which have a wide selection of bars.

### 10 Bars in Sancti Petri
MAP C6

Sip a cocktail and watch the sunset at one of the popular beach bars along the Costa de la Luz.

# Places to Eat in the Region

**PRICE CATEGORIES**

For a three-course meal for one with half a bottle of wine (or equivalent meal), taxes and extra charges.

€ under €30  €€ €30–€50  €€€ over €50

## 1 Ventorrillo del Chato, Cádiz

MAP B5 ■ Ctra Cádiz-San Fernando km 2 (Via Augusta Julia) ■ 956 25 00 25 ■ €€€

The oldest restaurant in Cádiz (1780) is also one of the best. Try *salmorejo*, a thick tomato soup served as a dip or side dish, and *dorada a la sal*, a local fish baked in a salt crust.

## 2 Antigua Casa de Guardia, Málaga

MAP Q5 ■ Alameda Principal 18 ■ 952 21 46 80 ■ Closed Sun ■ €

The city's oldest *taberna*, dating from 1840, has barrels of local wine in the bar. The steamed mussels are great.

Wine in Antigua Casa de Guardia

## 3 A Mar Restaurante, Jerez

MAP B5 ■ C/Latorre, 8 ■ 956 32 29 15 ■ €€

This small, trendy restaurant specializes in quality cuisine, with a particular focus on fresh seafood from the region.

## 4 Bar Juanito, Jerez

MAP B5 ■ C/Pescadería Vieja 8 & 10 ■ 956 33 48 38 ■ Closed Sun ■ €

Famous for the best tapas in town. It closes during the Feria in May.

## 5 Restaurante Los Portales, El Puerto de Santa María

MAP B5 ■ C/Ribera del Marisco 7 ■ 628 90 96 96 ■ €€

Savour traditional Cádiz delicacies in a renovated winery. Fish and seafood are the speciality here.

## 6 Sollo, Fuengirola

MAP D5 ■ Avda del Higuerón 48 ■ 951 38 56 22 ■ Closed L, Sun & Mon ■ €€€

Chef Diego Gallegos serves up unusual tapas-style dishes using snail caviar, eels, trout ceviche and ox-steak – all beautifully presented and complemented by superb coastal views.

## 7 Tragatá, Ronda

MAP D5 ■ C/Nueva 4 ■ 952 87 72 09 ■ €€

Former El Bulli chef Benito Gómez creates some of the best tapas in Andalucía. Stocks local Schatz organic wines.

## 8 Jardin del Califa, Vejer de la Frontera

MAP C6 ■ Plaza de España 12 ■ 956 45 17 06 ■ €€€

Truly exquisite North African and Middle Eastern cuisine is served in an enchanting complex of medieval buildings. Dine in the shady garden or a stone vaulted cellar.

## 9 Balandro, Cádiz

MAP B5 ■ Alameda Apodaca 22 ■ 956 22 09 92 ■ €€€

In an 18th-century mansion overlooking the bay, Balandro serves superb fried and grilled fish.

## 10 Restaurante Tropicana, Ronda

MAP D5 ■ C/Virgen de los Dolores 11 ■ 952 87 89 85 ■ Closed Mon & Tue ■ €€

Expect innovative takes on local and international dishes at this stylish restaurant.

*See map on pp102–3*

# **TOP 10** Granada and Almería Provinces

Enchanted by the beauty of Alhambra, arguably the pinnacle of Europe's Moorish palaces, visitors often forget to make time to see the area's other attractions. Besides Granada's many cultural landmarks, the entire region is worth exploring. Hikers will enjoy the mountain trails of the Sierra Nevada, beach-lovers will discover still unspoiled coastal areas and fans of Spaghetti Westerns will marvel at desert locations and movie film sets.

Urn, Cueva-Museo, Guadix

## 1 Guadix

MAP F4 ▪ Cueva-Museo: Plaza Padre Poveda; 958 66 55 67; open 10am–2pm & 4–6pm Mon–Fri, 10am–2pm Sat; adm; www.mcicuevas deguadix.blogspot.com

This ancient town is famous for its cave dwellings, inhabited for centuries. They were developed after the *reconquista* by local Moors who had been cast out of society by the Christians. The Barrio de las Cuevas is a surreal zone of brown hills with rounded whitewashed chimneys. To learn more, visit the Cueva-Museo or stay in a cave hotel *(see p146)*.

## 2 Capilla Real and Catedral, Granada

MAP Q2 ▪ Catedral: C/Gran Vía de Colón 5; open 10am–2pm & 3–7pm Mon–Sat; adm ▪ Capilla Real: C/Oficios 3; 958 22 78 48; open 10am–6:30pm Mon–Sat, 11am–6:30pm Sun; adm; www.capillarealgranada.com

To establish Christian rule, these triumphalist structures were built by some of the greatest architects of the age. The interior of Granada's cathedral is one of the most stunning achievements, while Alonso Cano's façade echoes the ancient triple arch favoured by Roman emperors. The Capilla Real (Royal Chapel) is

## GRANADA AND ALMERÍA PROVINCES

**Top 10 Sights** see pp116–19
**Restaurants** see p123
**Traditional Handicrafts** see p120
**Tearooms and Tapas Bars** see p122
**Nightlife** see p121

Granada's finest Christian building (*see p45*) and a repository of rare treasures, including a *reja* (gilded grille) by Bartolomé de Jaén, priceless jewels and paintings by Roger van der Weyden and Sandro Botticelli.

### 3 Alhama de Granada
MAP E4

Clinging precariously to the edge of a breathtaking gorge, this whitewashed village was known in Moorish times for its beauty and natural thermal waters (*al-hamma* means "hot spring" in Arabic). Hotel Balneario preserves an 11th-century *aljibe* (cistern), graced by Caliphal arches. In the 16th-century Iglesia de la Encarnación, some of the vestments are said to have been embroidered by Queen Isabel the Catholic.

### 4 Moorish Granada
MAP Q2 ▪ Museo CajaGRANADA: Memoria de Andalucía, Avda de la Ciencia 2; 958 22 22 57; open Sep–Jun: 9:30am–2pm Tue–Fri (also 4–7pm Fri), 10:30am–2pm Sat; Jul: 9:30am–2pm Mon–Fri; closed Sun, Mon & hols; adm; www.caja granadafundacion.es

The fairy-tale palace of the Alhambra (*see pp12–13*) draws millions of visitors each year. In the city below, the ancient Albaicín (*see pp16–17*) district embodies a microcosm of a Moroccan village, a "Little Morocco", with colourful market streets and tearooms. Behind the area stands Sacromonte, the traditional home of cave-dwelling Romas. Also worth a visit is the Museo CajaGRANADA, devoted to Andalucían culture.

**The magnificent Alhambra overlooking Granada**

**Late-winter skiing in the Sierra Nevada mountains**

### ⑤ Sierra Nevada

Spain's tallest peaks – and, after the Alps, Europe's second-loftiest chain – make Andalucía home to some excellent winter sports and robust trekking in spring and summer, as well as abundant wild flowers and wildlife. Stop in the historic villages of the Alpujarras, on the southern slopes, where time seems to have stood still, and see local artisans at work *(see pp38–9)*.

**Monasterio de la Cartuja, Granada**

### ⑥ Monasterio de la Cartuja, Granada

MAP F4 ■ Paseo de la Cartuja ■ 958 16 19 32 ■ Open summer: 10am–1pm & 4–8pm daily ■ Adm

Founded in 1516, this Carthusian monastery has a deceptively austere exterior considering the flamboyant Spanish Baroque detailing that can be found inside its church and sacristy. The busy flourishes and arabesques of polychromed and gilded stucco almost swallow up the architectural lines. The dazzling cupola by Antonio Palomino is a particular highlight.

### ⑦ "Wild West" Towns

MAP G4 ■ Fort Bravo: Ctra N340 km 468, Paraje de Unihay s/n, Tabernas; 902 07 08 14; open 9am–7:30pm daily; adm; www.fortbravo.org ■ Mini Hollywood: Ctra N340 km 464, Tabernas; 950 36 52 36; opening hours vary, check website for details; adm; www.oasysparquetematico.com

The interior of Almería Province resembles the deserts and canyons of the American Southwest: it was the perfect spot for filming the Wild West epics known as "Spaghetti Westerns" of the 1960s and 1970s. Two of the sets are now theme parks: Mini Hollywood *(see p71)* and Fort Bravo offer stunt shows and memorabilia. Here, visitors can re-enact classic film scenes or watch stuntpersons performing bank hold-ups or saloon brawls. These sets are occasionally used for TV ads and series.

### ⑧ Museo Parque de las Ciencias

MAP F4 ■ Avda de la Ciencia, Granada ■ 958 13 19 00 ■ Open 10am–7pm Tue–Sat, 10am–3pm Sun & hols ■ Adm ■ www.parqueciencias.com

This exciting complex *(see p53)*, dedicated to science and exploration, is made up of numerous interactive areas, such as Journey Through the Human Body, Perception, Eureka and Biosphere. There's an Observation Tower, a Planetarium and the Sala Explora, exclusively for children aged 3–7, where they can conduct their first experiments. There are temporary exhibitions too.

## PLASTICULTURA

If you approach the coastal area of these provinces from the west, you will notice the extent of plastic tenting, a phenomenon that reaches a peak before Almería. This agricultural technique is known as *plasticultura* and squeezes out every drop of moisture from these desert lands in order to produce crops. The process has raised environmental concerns and efforts are being made to make the recycling of plastic easier.

### ⑨ Almuñécar and Around

MAP F5 ■ Museo Arqueológico Cueva de Siete Palacios: Barrio de San Miguel; 958 61 61 31; opening hours vary, call ahead for details; adm

The Costa Tropical is a spectacular coast with towering mountains rising from the shore. Almuñécar is the chief town on this stretch and it is almost entirely devoted to resort life. Yet it has an ancient heritage, dating back to the Phoenicians, and was an important port under the Moors. The intriguing archaeological museum has a unique Egyptian vase dating from the 7th century BCE.

**Alcazaba, Almería**

### ⑩ Almería and Around

MAP G4 ■ Alcazaba: C/Almanzor; 950 80 10 08; open Tue–Sun; call ahead for opening hours; adm (free for EU members)

Almería, the "mirror of the sea", has lost much of its shine due to modern development. Still, its 10th-century Alcazaba is one of the most impressive surviving Moorish forts, and there are many spots with North African influences in the old quarter.

## A MORNING IN GRANADA

### ▶ MORNING

Begin your walk at Plaza Bib-Rambla, enhanced with flower stalls and the Neptune fountain. Fronting the western side of the square is the warren of ancient shopping streets called **La Alcaicería** *(see p120)*. Don't miss the 14th-century Moorish Corral del Carbón, which now houses a cultural centre.

Once the **cathedral** *(see pp116–17)* opens, it's time for a visit. Be sure to see the main chapel, a masterpiece by Siloé, and the ornaments and priceless treasures in the Chapter Room. The next stop is the **Capilla Real** *(see pp116–17)*; you should visit the crypt under the ostentatious marble sarcophagi of the kings and queens, where their bodies repose in plain lead boxes. On the carved Renaissance sepulchres, note the split pomegranate, symbol of a defeated Moorish Granada.

Continue on across the busy thoroughfares until you get to the river and the long expanse of **Plaza Nueva** *(see p59)*. Choose an outside table (the cafés here are all similar), order a drink and take in the street life.

It's time to enter the labyrinth of the **Albaicín** *(see pp16–17)*. Take Calle Elvira up to Calle Calderería Vieja for the vibrant bazaar of the Moorish Quarter. Following the old steep streets, keep going until you reach the fanciful **La Tetería del Bañuelo** *(see p122)*, an inviting place to sip some mint tea and sample Moroccan sweets.

See map on pp116–17 ←

# Traditional Handicrafts

### ① Albaicín, Granada

The rustic Moroccan shops in this ancient quarter *(see pp16–17)* are all concentrated on two sloping streets off Calle Elvira – Calderería Vieja and Calderería Nueva.

### ② Cerámica Miguel Muñoz, Granada

MAP Q2 ▪ Plaza Pescadería 10 ▪ 958 28 81 92

This traditional ceramics store sells the typical style of the region: blue patterns on white tiles, often with a pomegranate motif.

### ③ Taracea Laguna, Granada

MAP S2 ▪ Real de la Alhambra 30 ▪ 958 22 90 19

Opposite the entrance to the Alhambra, you can see how *taracea* (Moorish marquetry, often inlaid with bone, mother of pearl or silver) is made, and take home a souvenir unique to this area.

### ④ Al Aire Art, Granada

MAP R1 ▪ Plaza Aliatar 16 ▪ 622 36 46 51

Located in the Albaicín area, this small shop features high-quality handmade artworks.

### ⑤ El Rocío, Granada

MAP Q2 ▪ C/Capuchinas 8 ▪ 958 26 58 23

The complete outfitter for *romería* and festival-going gear. All the frills, polka dots and bright colours will dazzle your eye, and it all comes in every size, so even babies can have a flounce or two.

### ⑥ Bazar el Valenciano, Almería

MAP G4 ▪ C/Las Tiendas 34 ▪ 950 23 45 93

This is the oldest store in town. Look for "El Indalo" souvenirs, which are items bearing the symbol of Almería for good luck.

### ⑦ Carrera de la Virgen, Granada

MAP F4 ▪ Ibérica: Carrera de la Virgen 44 ▪ Abuela Ili: Carrera de la Virgen 51

This street has some great gourmet shops. Ibérica, a deli specializing in local fare, is a must-try, while Abuela Ili is a specialist chocolate shop best suited to those with a sweet tooth.

### ⑧ La Alcaicería, Granada

MAP Q2

In Moorish times this was the silk market, although the horseshoe arches and stucco are a modern re-creation. The narrow alleyways are bursting with colourful wares such as silver jewellery, embroidered silk shawls and ceramics.

**Narrow alleys of La Alcaicería**

### ⑨ Alpujarras Crafts

MAP F4–G4

The hill towns of this zone are rich in traditional crafts, including ceramics and weaving. Local *jarapas* (rugs), bags, ponchos and blankets are hand-loomed in age-old patterns. They're sold at local weekly markets.

### ⑩ Níjar, Almería Province

MAP H4

This coastal town is known for its distinctive pottery and *jarapas*. Head for Calle Las Eras, in the Barrio Alfarero, to find the genuine article.

# Nightlife

### 1 La Canastera, Almería

Enjoy Flamenco performances at this venue in the Pescadería neighbourhood of Almería (see p51). Shows are held every Thursday and Saturday evening with tickets selling around €20. Only cash is accepted.

### 2 Sala Vogue
**MAP Q1 ■ C/Duquesa 39 ■ www.festgra.com/discoteca/sala-vogue**

This trendy nightclub in the Realejo district is an indie favourite. There are two rooms, with different vibes and DJs.

### 3 TragoFino-San Matias 30, Granada
**MAP Q2 ■ Plaza de las Descalzas 3 ■ 665 40 93 12**

This trendy bar, located in the heart of Granada, is a popular spot with the locals. It serves a variety of reasonably priced, delicious cocktails. The service is friendly and attentive.

### 4 Eurostars Gran Vía, Granada
**MAP Q1 ■ C/Gran Vía de Colón, 20 ■ 958 21 78 10**

Enjoy a cocktail on the terrace with great views of the Seville Cathedral and the Alhambra. Indoor and outdoor zones make this a perfect place to visit all year round.

### 5 Planta Baja, Granada
**MAP F4 ■ C/Horno de Abad 11 ■ www.plantabaja.club**

A two-storey venue: the upper floor is a quiet bar; downstairs, the DJs play chart hits and everyone dances. There is live music on the weekends.

### 6 Abanicos, Almería
**MAP G5 ■ C/Goya 2, 04648 Pulpí ■ www.abanicosterreros.com**

This summer-only bar specializes in cocktails served with a tropical flair.

**Outdoor seating at El Camborio**

### 7 El Camborio, Granada
**MAP S1 ■ Camino del Sacromonte 47 ■ 679 88 58 94 ■ Closed Sun & Mon**

This is a popular night venue in the caves of Sacromonte (see p17). Music echoes from four dance floors to the rooftop terraces, offering a striking view of the Alhambra at sunrise.

### 8 Chaplin's Pub, Almería
**MAP G5 ■ Calle Sierra Nevada 27, Roquetas de Mar ■ 618 82 43 68 ■ Closed Mon–Wed ■ www.chaplinspub.business.site**

Watch sporting events, play bar games and enjoy a pint of beer at this classic British pub.

### 9 Maui Beach, Almería
**MAP H4 ■ Paseo del Mediterráneo 40, Mojácar Beach ■ 950 47 87 22**

This charming chiringuito (beach bar) offers a variety of zones, each with a great ambience. At night, Maui Beach transforms from a bar-cum-restaurant into a lively club.

### 10 Hanalei Cocktail Bar, Granada
**MAP Q3 ■ C/Piedra Santa, 22 ■ 622 47 68 00 ■ www.grupoparipe.com/hanalei**

Inspired by a fusion of flavours from Polynesia, Brazil and the Caribbean, the Tiki cocktails served at Hanalei will not disappoint.

*See map on pp116–17*

# Tearooms and Tapas Bars

### 1 La Tetería del Bañuelo, Granada
MAP R2 ■ C/Bañuelo 5

A more relaxed and inviting place is hard to imagine. The little rooms and intimate niches are suffused with a gentle light, the air with the aromas of tea and flowers and the sound of songbirds. Try sweets and fragrant brews, and enjoy unsurpassed views.

### 2 Kasbah, Granada
MAP Q2 ■ C/Calderería Nueva 4

Relax amid the comforts of this candlelit café. Silky pillows and romantic nooks abound. You can taste Arab pastries and a selection of Moroccan teas.

Casa Puga, a traditional tapas bar

### 3 Casa Puga, Almería
MAP G4 ■ C/Jovellanos 7 ■ Closed Sun

One of the city's best tapas bars. The wine list is exhaustive, as you might guess from the wine racks on view.

### 4 Bar La Buena Vida, Granada
MAP Q2 ■ C/Almiceros 12

A welcoming tapas bar with a good variety of wines and beers. There's free tapas with each drink, so you can sample a wide variety of treats without breaking the bank.

### 5 La Riviera, Granada
MAP Q2 ■ C/Cetti Meriem 7

Located in the heart of the city, La Riviera offers a good variety of beer and tapas.

### 6 Antigua Bodega Castañeda, Granada
MAP Q2 ■ C/Elvira 5

Antique wine barrels and hanging hams give a rustic feel. The cheese boards are a good bet, as are the *montaditos* (small sandwiches).

### 7 Casa Enrique, Granada
MAP Q3 ■ C/Acero de Darro 8 ■ Closed Sun D

Another wonderfully old-fashioned hole-in-the-wall lined with antique barrels. Try the *montaditos de lomo* (small sandwiches with pork fillet) and *torta del casar* (sheep's-milk cheese).

### 8 Tetería Al Hammam Almeraya, Almería
MAP G4 ■ C/Perea 9 ■ Closed Mon & Tue

Escape from the crowds and head for the tranquil tearoom of Almería's Arab baths, where you can enjoy Moorish-inspired teas and snacks.

### 9 Bodega Francisco, Almuñécar
MAP F5 ■ C/Real 11

A forest of ham shanks hanging from the ceiling greets the eye, along with barrels of *fino* in this traditional tapas bar. The attached restaurant next door, Francisco II, serves full meals.

### 10 El Quinto Toro, Almería
MAP G4 ■ Juan Leal 6 ■ Closed Mon–Wed D; Sat D & Sun

The name derives from the tradition that the best bull of a *corrida* is chosen to fight in the fifth (*quinto*) confrontation of the day. This tapas bar is favoured by local aficionados of the bullfight.

# Restaurants

### 1 Cunini, Granada
MAP F4 ▪ Plaza Pescadería 14 ▪ 958 25 07 77 ▪ Closed Sun D, Mon ▪ €€

The fresh seafood, brought in daily from Motril, is highly recommended, and is a big hit with the food critics.

**PRICE CATEGORIES**
For a three-course meal for one with half a bottle of wine (or equivalent meal), taxes and extra charges.

€ under €30  €€ €30–€50  €€€ over €50

**Arrayanes Moroccan restaurant**

### 2 Arrayanes, Granada
MAP Q2 ▪ Cuesta Marañas 4 ▪ 958 22 84 01 ▪ Closed Tue ▪ €

A sophisticated Moroccan restaurant serving tagines, couscous and pastries. Halal meat and no alcohol.

### 3 Carmen Mirador de Aixa, Granada
MAP R2 ▪ Carril de San Agustín 2 ▪ 958 04 98 10 ▪ €€€

Enjoy excellent interpretations of regional dishes such as habas con jamón (broad beans with ham).Views of the Alhambra from the terrace.

### 4 Restaurante El Ventorro, Alhama de Granada
MAP E4 ▪ Ctra de Jatar km 2 ▪ 958 35 04 38 ▪ Closed Mon ▪ €€

In this lovely rural restaurant you can try Grandma Currilla's potato stew, as well as sumptuous casseroles and grilled meat.

### 5 Restaurante González, Trevélez
MAP F4 ▪ Plaza Francisco Abellán ▪ 958 85 85 33 ▪ €€

Perfect spot to try the flavourful ham that the region is known for, while taking in the scenic views.

### 6 El Chaleco, Almuñécar
MAP F5 ▪ Avda Costa del Sol 37 ▪ 958 63 24 02 ▪ Closed Sun D, Mon (except Jul & Aug) ▪ €€

French cuisine, lovingly prepared with attention to detail, is served in a romantic, intimate setting.

### 7 Restaurante Mar De Plata, Almuñecar
MAP F5 ▪ Avda Mar de Plata 3 ▪ 958 63 30 79 ▪ €

At this Mediterranean restaurant choose from a wide selection of dishes, particularly focused on fresh fish and seafood. Do not miss arroz con bogavante (rice with lobster).

### 8 Pesetas, Salobreña
MAP F5 ▪ C/Bóveda 11 ▪ 958 61 01 82 ▪ Closed Mon & Tue ▪ €

Absorb the ambience of the old quarters of Salobreña and the excellent views of the coast while dining here. The choco a la marinera (squid in tomato sauce) is a speciality. Good salads, too.

### 9 Restaurante Valentín, Almería
MAP G4 ▪ C/Tenor Iribarne 19 ▪ 950 26 44 75 ▪ Closed Mon, Sep ▪ €

Specialities at Restaurante Valentín include highly delectable arroz negro (rice in squid ink) and pescado en adobo (marinated fish).

### 10 La Goleta, San Miguel del Cabo de Gata
MAP H5 ▪ Paseo Marítimo Cabo de Gata ▪ 950 37 02 15 ▪ Closed Mon, first 2 weeks in Nov ▪ €€

All the seafood is at its freshest here, of course, since this village is located right in the middle of Andalucía's most unspoiled coast.

*See map on pp116–17*

# TOP 10 Córdoba and Jaén Provinces

These two provinces are an attractive blend of exquisite urban architecture, famed agricultural zones and great wildlife reserves within rugged mountain ranges. The ancient treasure-trove of Córdoba is the star, but the Renaissance towns of Baeza and Úbeda are among the region's most beautiful. For lovers of delicious wine, ham and olive oil, the areas around Montilla, Valle de los Pedroches and

**Iberian art, Museo Provincial de Jaén**

Baena should not be missed. Meanwhile, nature lovers can hike for days amid the wilds of the Parque Natural de la Sierra de Cardeña y Montoro in Córdoba and the Sierra de Cazorla in Jaén.

**Alcázar, Córdoba**

## 1 Córdoba

This town (see pp22–5), wonderfully rich in history and cultural importance, is also small enough to cover easily and enjoyably on foot. It has a delightfully contrasting mix of sights, from the architectural splendour of the great mosque – with a Christian church oddly sprouting out of its centre – to the whitewashed glories of the old Jewish quarter, the splendid Alcázar and the Zoco

### CÓRDOBA AND JAÉN PROVINCES

Municipal with its diverse selection of goods made by local artists. There are engaging museums as well, featuring works of art by Old Masters and local artists, and ancient artifacts evoking the area's influential past.

### 2 Úbeda

Ignore the downtrodden outskirts as you approach this town (see p35) – once you get to the historic centre you will realize that it is one of Andalucía's most remarkable splendours. The keynote here is architecture – an entire district of Renaissance edifices built for local nobility in the 16th century. One of Andalucía's greatest architects, Andrés de Vandelvira, was the genius who gave most of these structures their harmonious forms.

### 3 Baeza

Like nearby Úbeda, this smaller town (see p34) is also a jewel of Renaissance glory, but includes earlier remains dating back to the Moors and, before them, the Romans. The town radiates a sense of tranquillity as you walk from one cluster of lovely buildings to another. Again, much of the beauty owes its existence to the architect Andrés de Vandelvira.

**Ruins of Medina Azahara palace**

### 4 Medina Azahara

MAP D3 ▪ Ctra Palma del Río km 5.5, W of Córdoba ▪ 957 10 49 33 ▪ Opening hours vary, check website for details ▪ Adm (free for EU members) ▪ www.medinaazahara.org

The building of the first palace here dates from 936 CE, commissioned by Caliph Abd ar-Rahman III, Emir of Córdoba and the man who brought the city to glory. He named it after his favourite wife, Az-Zahra (the Radiant). Though it is little more than a ruin now, at one time it held a zoo, ponds and gardens, baths, houses, barracks, markets, mosques, a harem of 6,000 women and accommodation for 4,000 enslaved people. Nighttime visits are available in the spring and summer months, providing a magical experience.

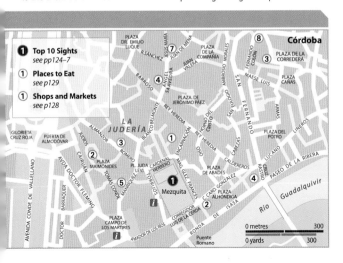

Córdoba

0 metres 300
0 yards 300

### 5 Montoro

MAP E2 ■ Museo Arqueológico: Plaza de Santa María de la Mota; 957 16 23 00; open May–Sep: 9:30am–1:30pm daily; Oct–Apr: 10am–2pm daily ■ Casa de las Conchas: C/Criado 17; 957 16 00 89 (tourist office); tours operate Sat & Sun; adm

Laid out on an undulating series of five hills at a bend in the river, this ancient town sports a Baroque tower and a handsome 15th-century bridge. Other sights include a good Museo Arqueológico Municipal and the eccentrically kitsch Casa de las Conchas, a shell-encrusted folly; contact the tourist office for a tour.

### 6 Cástulo

MAP F2 ■ Ctra Linares-Torrreblascopedro (JV-3003) km 3.3 ■ 953 106 074 ■ Opening hours vary, check website for details ■ Adm (free for EU members) ■ Monographic Museum of Cástulo: Calle General Echagüe 2, 23700 Linares; 953 60 93 89; opening hours vary, check website for details; www.museosdeandalucia.es

The ruins of this ancient city are situated in a strategic position in the Guadalquivir Valley. Cástulo is open to the public and is home to some immaculately preserved mosaics. The Monographic Museum of Cástulo, dedicated to this city and its history, is located 7 km away in Linares.

### 7 Castillo de Almodóvar

MAP D3 ■ Almodóvar del Río 25 km (16 miles) W of Córdoba ■ 957 63 40 55 ■ Opening hours vary, check website for details ■ www.castillodealmodovar.com ■ Adm

Originally the site of a Roman, then a Moorish, fortification, the present

**BAENA OLIVE OIL**

This Córdoba Province town is famed for its olive oil, and you can catch its unmistakable fragrance as you enter the district. The Museo del Olivar y el Aceite (C/Cañada 7; 957 69 16 41; open Tue–Sun) is well worth a visit (above). It shows how each organically grown olive is carefully kept from bruising and the paste is extracted by the process of stone crushing.

castle goes back to the 1300s, when it was embellished in Gothic style. Legend holds that ghosts of those who died while imprisoned here haunt the eight monolithic towers.

### 8 Montilla

MAP D3 ■ Bodegas Alvear: Avda de María Auxiliadora 1; 957 65 01 00; open Mon–Sat for tours in English, by appt; adm; www.alvear.es

The centre of Córdoba's wine-making region, this town gave *amontillado* sherry its name (it means "in the style of Montilla"). The wine here is like sherry, but nuttier and more toasted. Since the region is hotter than around Jerez, the grapes ripen more intensely and the wines need no fortifying. You can taste the difference at Bodegas Alvear (see p76), founded in 1729.

**Castillo de Almodóvar**

## ⑨ Jaén

MAP E3 ■ Cathedral: Plaza Santa María; open 10am–2:30pm & 4:30–8:30pm Mon–Fri, 10am–8:30pm Sat, 10am–11:30pm & 4–8pm Sun; adm ■ Museo Provincial de Jaén: Paseo de la Estación 29; open Jul–Aug: 9am–3pm Tue–Sun; mid-Sep–Jun: 9am–9pm Tue–Sat, 9am–3pm Sun; adm (free for EU members)

This modern provincial capital is set off by the dramatically placed ramparts of the mighty Castillo de Santa Catalina (see p47) and the immensity of its double-towered cathedral by Vandelvira (see p45). You can experience the castle and its spectacular views of the city and surrounding olive groves, as it now houses a parador. The Museo Provincial de Jaén houses the country's finest collection of 5th-century BCE Iberian sculpture.

**Castillo de Santa Catalina, Jaén**

## ⑩ Alcalá La Real

MAP E3 ■ Fortress: 953 10 27 17 ■ Open Apr–mid-Oct: 10:30am–7:30pm daily; mid-Oct–Mar: 10am–6pm daily ■ Adm

The 12th-century Fortaleza de la Mota (see p46) dominates this once strategic town and is unique in Jaén Province in that its original Moorish castle was built by Badis Aben Habuz, the ruler of Granada. Mostly in ruins, it still pre-serves the original seven gates. Inside, built on the remains of a mosque, is the Gothic-Mudéjar church of Santo Domingo, which uses the former minaret as a bell tower.

---

### A MORNING WALK THROUGH BAEZA

Paseo de la Constitución
Torre de los Aliatares
Taberna El Pájaro
La Alhóndiga
Iglesia de Santa Cruz
Fuente de los Leones
Plaza del Pópulo
Puerta de Jaén
Palacio de Jabalquinto
Plaza Santa María
Cathedral

#### ▶ MORNING

Your tour of this Renaissance town starts at the lovely **Plaza del Pópulo** (see p34). The tourist office is inside a fine Plateresque palace, the Casa del Pópulo. Next to it are the arches of the **Puerta de Jaén** (see p34) and the Arco de Villalar, and in the centre is the Fuente de los Leones. The ruined lions and their eroded mistress, said to be a statue of Hannibal's wife, still manage to convey an undeniable elegance.

Exiting the square to the left of the tourist office, continue southeast to the **Plaza Santa María** (see p34) and the **cathedral**. Inside the cathedral, don't miss the extravagant choir screen by Bartolomé de Jaén.

Next stop, to the north, is the **Palacio de Jabalquinto** (see p34), with one of the most eccentric façades in the region, an example of Isabelline Plateresque style. It is now a university but you can still go and visit its inner patio, then that of the Antigua Universidad next door. Opposite the palace, admire the **Iglesia de Santa Cruz** (see p26), a well-preserved church from the 13th century.

Down the street, you can see the 1,000-year-old Moorish Torre de los Aliatares and around the corner, facing **Paseo de la Constitución** (see p34), La Alhóndiga, the old corn exchange, with its triple-tiered façade.

Have lunch at traditional **Taberna El Pájaro** (Portales Tundidores 5; 953 74 43 48; closed Mon), with its rustic stone walls, local fare and extensive wine list.

See map on pp124–5 ⟵

# Shops and Markets

**Meryan leather workshop**

### 1 Meryan, Córdoba
MAP D3 ▪ Calleja de las Flores 2 ▪ 957 47 59 02

Specialists in hand-tooled leather goods; pick up a souvenir from your visit – from handbags, accessories and frames to furniture.

### 2 Zoco Municipal, Córdoba
MAP D3 ▪ C/Judíos s/n ▪ 957 29 05 75

This historic house and patio has been converted into a co-op for local artists working in ceramics, leather, metalworks and woodwork.

### 3 Kuvo Plata, Córdoba
MAP D3 ▪ C/Rodríguez Marín 18 ▪ 957 485 552 ▪ www.kuvoplata.com

Located in the heart of Córdoba, close to the Templo Romano, this shop sells traditional silver jewellery inspired by Córdoba's history and culture.

### 4 La Oleoteca, Córdoba
MAP D3 ▪ C/Ángel de Saavedra 8 ▪ 957 24 41 01 ▪ www.laoleoteca.org

Gourmet store specializing in extra virgin olive oil and other regional products sourced from the local producers. Tasting and sampling of products is encouraged.

### 5 Baraka, Córdoba
MAP D3 ▪ C/Manríquez ▪ 957 48 83 27

This is a good spot for quality souvenirs. Choose from ceramics, leather goods, glassware and other accessories, all handmade.

### 6 Ubedíes Artesanía con Esparto, Úbeda
MAP F2 ▪ C/Real 45–7 ▪ 639 56 37 88 ▪ www.artesaniaconesparto.com

Here you'll find an innovative selection of items made with esparto grass, ranging from shoes to decorative items.

### 7 Monsieur Bourguignon, Córdoba
MAP D3 ▪ C/Jesús María 11 ▪ 605 98 75 84

A decadent shop offering an assortment of chocolates, biscuits and handmade sweets, which are almost too pretty to eat.

### 8 Galería de Vinos Caldos, Jaén
MAP E3 ▪ C/Ceron 12 ▪ 953 23 59 99

One of the area's best, this wine shop stocks regional wines, including those from Montilla (see p126).

### 9 Pottery Quarter, Úbeda
MAP F2 ▪ C/Valencia

Úbeda is famous for its dark green pottery, fired in wood kilns over olive stones. Its intricate, pierced designs are Moorish-inspired and the workmanship superb.

**Intricate green Úbeda pottery**

### 10 Flea Market, Jaén
MAP E3 ▪ Recinto Ferial, Avda de Granada

Thursday mornings see this street come to life with a catch-all market that can net you anything from pure junk to a rare treasure.

# Places to Eat

## 1 Restaurante & Bistró Casa Alfonso, Cazorla

MAP G3 ▪ Placeta Consuelo Mendieta 2 ▪ 953 72 14 63 ▪ Closed Tue ▪ €€

Expertly prepared dishes and attentive service are on offer at this restaurant with an elegant setting. Try one of the taster menus *(menu de degustación)*.

## 2 Horno San Luis, Córdoba

MAP D3 ▪ C/Cardenal Gonzalez 73 ▪ 957 47 45 29 ▪ €€

Housed in a historic *panaderia* (bread bakery), this stylish restaurant serves a varied cuisine.

## 3 El Churrasco, Córdoba

MAP D3 ▪ C/Romero 16 ▪ 957 29 08 19 ▪ Closed Aug ▪ €€€

One of the city's smartest, this restaurant serves sumptuous traditional fare. Sample the eponymous *churrasco* (grilled pork loin with spicy red pepper sauce).

## 4 Almudaina, Córdoba

MAP D3 ▪ Plaza Campo Santo de los Martires 1 ▪ 957 47 43 42 ▪ Closed Sun D ▪ €€

Set in a 16th-century mansion, this is another great place to try traditional dishes, such as *pechuga de perniz en salsa* (partridge breasts in sauce).

## 5 Xavi Taberna, Baeza

MAP F2 ▪ Portales Tundidores 8 ▪ 953 82 33 39 ▪ Closed Wed ▪ €€

An excellent choice of seafood, plus a number of vegetarian dishes, are available at this centrally located restaurant. There is also an extensive and reasonably priced wine list. The service is friendly and attentive.

## 6 Casa Rubio, Córdoba

MAP E3 ▪ C/Puerta de Almodóvar, 5 ▪ 957 42 08 53 ▪ Closed Tue ▪ €€

This Michelin-star restaurant serves a combination of nouvelle cuisine with the traditional flavours of the region.

## 7 Las Camachas, Montilla

MAP D3 ▪ Ctra Madrid-Málaga, Avda de Europa 3 ▪ 957 65 00 04 ▪ €€

Fish dishes are a speciality; opt for the hake loin with clams and prawns, paired with the delightful local wine.

The popular Taberna Salinas

## 8 Taberna Salinas, Córdoba

MAP D3 ▪ C/Tundidores 3 ▪ 957 48 29 50 ▪ Closed Sun D & Mon ▪ €

A bustling place, with dining rooms around a patio. Try the *naranjas picás con aceite y bacalao* (cod with orange and olive oil).

## 9 Panaceite, Jaén

MAP E3 ▪ C/Bernabe Soriano 1 ▪ 953 24 06 30 ▪ €

If you're looking for a good selection of local specialities, head to Panaceite. Try the pork loin with onion marmalade.

## 10 Mesón Navarro, Úbeda

MAP F2 ▪ Plaza Ayuntamiento 2 ▪ 953 75 73 95 ▪ Closed Tue ▪ €

Try the *pinchitos* (kebabs) and *ochios* (rolls) at this local institution.

See map on pp124–5

# Streetsmart

Walking through an alley with
whitewashed houses in Málaga

# Getting Around

## Arriving by Air

Andalucía is served by **airports** in Málaga, Almería, Granada-Jaén, Jerez and Seville.

Málaga–Costa del Sol Airport (AGP) is Spain's fourth busiest, with frequent scheduled and charter connections to many European cities and seasonal services to Canada and the US. Buses run from the airport to Marbella (45 minutes, €6.15). Trains depart every 20 minutes on Line C1 for the María Zambrano station in Málaga, which is 14 km (8.6 miles) away; a one-way ticket costs €1.80 and the journey takes 8 minutes. In the opposite direction, the C1 stops at Torre-molinos, Benalmádena and Fuengirola.

The much smaller Almería (LEI), Federico García Lorca Granada-Jaén (GRX), Jerez de Frontera (XRY) and Seville (SVQ) airports are served by domestic as well as European airlines, with chartered services increasing in the summer months. There are excellent public transport links from the airports to their nearest cities.

Gibraltar (GIB) airport operates flights to UK airports and to Morocco.

## International Train Travel

Spain's international and domestic rail services are operated by state-run Red Nacional de Ferrocarriles Españoles (**Renfe**).

Safety and hygiene measures, timetables, ticket information, transport maps, and more can be obtained from the Renfe website. For international train trips, it is advisable to purchase your ticket well in advance. **Eurail** sells passes (to European non-residents and residents respectively), which are valid on Renfe trains.

International train services terminate in either Barcelona or Madrid, from where you can catch a domestic service to Andalucía. Trains from London, Brussels, Amsterdam, Geneva, Paris, Zürich and Milan reach Barcelona via Cerbère. At Cerbère, you can connect to the Tren Articulado Ligero Goicoechea Oriol (TALGO), a high-speed luxury train service (operated by Renfe).

There are two main rail routes from Portugal to Spain. The Sud Express departs daily from Lisbon and terminates in the French town of Hendaye, from where you can catch one of the regular services to Madrid. Alternatively, Lusitania is a sleeper train from Lisbon, which will take you to Madrid in around nine hours.

## Regional and Local Trains

Renfe, along with some regional companies, operates a good train service throughout Andalucía. You can buy tickets online on the individual operators'

websites or at stations. The fastest intercity services are the TALGO, Iryo, Avlo (Renfe's low-cost train line) and AVE (Renfe's full-service line), which link Madrid with Seville in two and a half hours. High-speed routes also link Barcelona with Seville and Málaga – both trips take five and a half hours. As a guide, a one-way *turista* (second-class) ticket from Madrid to Málaga starts at €18 (Iryo) or €25.45 (AVE).

The *largo recorrido* (long-distance) trains are cheaper than the high-speed trains, but they are so slow that you usually need to travel overnight. Book at least a month in advance. *Regionales y cercanías* (the regional and local services) are frequent and cheap.

## Long-Distance Bus Travel

Often the cheapest and easiest way to reach and travel around Andalucía is by coach. Coaches run frequently between major cities and towns in Andalucía, and connect the region to the rest of Spain. The major coach stations in Andalucía are in Seville, Córdoba, Granada, Málaga and Almería. **Eurolines** links Andalucía to Portugal and there are also international links to France, the Netherlands, Belgium, Switzerland and Austria.

Spain has no national coach company, but private regional companies operate routes around the country. The largest of these is **Alsa**. Other companies operate in particular regions – Alsina Graells, for instance, covers most of the south and east of Spain. The modern buses are comfortable, clean, air-conditioned and also tend to offer WI-Fi.

For short journeys, tickets can be bought from the driver when boarding the bus. For medium- to long-distance travel, you can make reservations at bus stations, or online via **Movelia**, as well as from individual bus companies. Note that it is not always possible to book tickets for long-distance travel in advance.

## Public Transport

Sightseeing and getting around Andalucía is best done on foot and by public transport. In most towns and cities, bus services suffice as the sole means of public transport; Seville, Málaga and Granada also have tram and metro systems. Jaén has the infrastructure for a tram system, which is meant to be running in 2024. Municipal or tourism websites in **Córdoba**, **Seville**, **Granada**, **Málaga**, **Almería** and **Cádiz** offer up-to-date information about their public transport options.

## Tickets

The best place to purchase public transport tickets is at stations themselves, either from windows or automatic machines. They are also available at newsagents. They come either in the form of a physical ticket or as a smart card which can either hold a season ticket or be topped up with cash and used pay-as-you-go.

## Metro

The **Metro de Sevilla** was designed to aid transport between the outer areas of Seville and the city centre. The system will eventually consist of four metro lines, which will provide easy access to bus and train stations.

The **Metro de Málaga** has two lines, which connect the outer suburbs to Guadalmedina and Atarazanas stations in the city centre.

The **Metropolitano de Granada** connects central Granada with the towns Armilla, Albolote and Maracena.

## Trams

Seville's city centre operates a tram system called the MetroCentro. It provides air-conditioned, rapid transport between San Bernardo station and Plaza Nueva in an otherwise pedestrian-only zone. An extension to the line is due to open late 2023, which will extend the network to Puerta Osorio and Santa Justa train station.

Pay at the machine at tram stops (or pass your smart card over the reader on board) and press the green button to open the door. MetroCentro trams run every 3 to 5 minutes and stop briefly at all stops.

---

### DIRECTORY

**ARRIVING BY AIR**

**Airports**
📞 91 321 10 00
🌐 aena.es (which operates all Spain's main airports)

**INTERNATIONAL TRAIN TRAVEL**

**Avlo**
🌐 avlorenfe.com

**Eurail**
🌐 eurail.com

**Iryo**
🌐 iryo.eu

**Renfe**
🌐 renfe.com

**LONG-DISTANCE BUS TRAVEL**

**Alsa**
🌐 alsa.es

**Eurolines**
🌐 eurolines.com

**Movelia**
🌐 movelia.es

**PUBLIC TRANSPORT**

**Almería**
🌐 almeriaciudad.es

**Cádiz**
🌐 tranviadecadizasanfernandoycarraca.es

**Córdoba**
🌐 cordoba.es

**Granada**
🌐 movilidadgranada.com

**Málaga**
🌐 movilidadmalaga.eu

**Seville**
🌐 visitasevilla.es

**METRO**

**Metropolitano de Granada**
🌐 metropolitanogranada.es

**Metro de Málaga**
🌐 metromalaga.es

**Metro de Sevilla**
🌐 metro-sevilla.es

## Bus

Buses remain the most common mode of public transport throughout Andalucía, and are the easiest and cheapest way to get around Seville's main sights. However, they can sometimes follow an erratic timetable and many services do not run after 10pm.

Bus routes can be found on the **TUSSAM** website but, generally speaking, the most useful lines for visitors are the circulares, numbered C1 to C6, which run around the city centre. In Granada, C30, C32 and C35 run from the centre to the Albaicín, Alhambra and Sacromonte.

## Taxis

Throughout Andalucía, particularly in cities and towns, taxis are a reasonably priced way to get around if public transport isn't an option. Generally speaking, the journey starts with a flat fee and then increases depending on the distance travelled. Fares tend to be higher at night and also during the weekend and public holidays. Surcharges usually apply for trips to airports, and bus and train stations.

For a more affordable option, visitors can use ridesharing services, such as **BlaBlaCar**, to travel between cities.

Málaga is famous for its Bike Taxis or Trixis. Passengers sit in a pod-like carriage, towed along behind a bicycle. You are completely covered, so it can be an all-weather travel option.

## Driving

If you drive to Spain in your own car, you must carry the vehicle's registration document, a valid insurance certificate, a passport or a national identity card, and your driving licence at all times. You must also display a sticker on the back of the car showing its country of registration. Note that you risk on-the-spot fines if you do not carry a red warning triangle and a reflective jacket with you at all times.

Spain has two different types of motorway: *autopistas*, which are toll roads, and *autovías*, which are toll-free. You can establish whether a motorway is toll-free by the letters that prefix the number of the road: A = free; AP = toll motorway.

*Carreteras nacionales*, Spain's main roads, have black-and-white signs and are designated by the letter N (Nacional) plus a number. Those with Roman numerals start at the Puerta del Sol in Madrid, and those with ordinary numbers have kilometre markers giving the distance from the provincial capital.

*Carreteras comarcales*, secondary roads, have a number preceded by the letter C. Other minor roads have numbers preceded by letters representing the name of the province, such as the LE1313 in Lleida.

Parking can be difficult, especially in the *pueblos blancos* where the roads are narrow and there is limited availability. Instead, park outside the old town areas and walk in.

From 2024, access to most Spanish cities with over 50,0000 inhabitants will be restricted. City centres will be off-limits to vehicles that do not meet the emissions restrictions or do not display a government issued emissions sticker.

## Car Hire

In Andalucía all airports have several providers and there are many more smaller companies operating in the city centres. To hire a car you'll need a valid full driving licence, passport and credit card; some agencies will only accept customers over 21 or even 25 years.

The most popular car-hire companies in Spain are **Europcar**, **Avis** and **Hertz**. Fly-drive, an option for two or more travellers where car hire is included in the cost of your airfare, can be arranged by travel agents and tour operators. If you wish to hire a car locally for around a week or less, you will be able to arrange it with a local travel agent. A car for hire is called a *coche de alquiler*.

## Rules of the Road

When using a car in Spain, drive on the right and use the left lane only for passing other vehicles.

If you have taken the wrong road, and it has a solid white line, turn round as indicated by a *cambio de sentido* sign. At crossings, give way to all on-coming traffic, unless a sign indicates otherwise.

The speed limit is 120 km/h (74 mph) on highways and dual

carriageways, 100 km/h (62 mph) on roads with more than one lane in each direction and 90 km/h (55 mph) on all other ordinary roads, unless otherwise indicated. In urban areas, the speed can be as low as 20 km/h (12 mph).

The blood-alcohol concentration (BAC) limit for drivers of private vehicles and cyclists is 0.5 mg/ml and is strictly enforced. After a traffic accident, all those involved have to undergo a breath test. The **RAC** has further information for driving in Spain.

## Boats and Ferries

Ferries connect the Spanish mainland to the Balearic and Canary Islands, and to North Africa, Italy and the UK. All the important routes are served by car ferries. **Acciona Trasmediterránea** operates a weekly service from Cádiz to the main ports of the Canary Islands. Always make an advance booking, especially in summer.

## Cycling

There are cycle lanes in most Andalucían cities. Seville has pedestrianized a main thoroughfare in the centre, creating a wide promenade, which allows for bikes. Rural Andalucía is bicycle-friendly, with an extensive network of back roads, though steep inclines can be testing for inexperienced cyclists.

For easier cycling, try the **Via Verde** – "Greenway" – established throughout Spain by converting

unused railway lines into recreational areas for leisure cycling, walking and horse riding. There are routes through each province in Andalucía. Bike hire is available in all the main towns and cities.

**SEVICI** is a self-service bike rental programme in Seville, with 2,500 bikes available 24 hours a day. Bikes can be hired free for 30 minutes and are charged per hour after that. Daily, weekly and annual rental subscriptions can be purchased online or through the app.

Motorists tend to treat cyclists as a nuisance and city traffic can be dangerous for cyclists. Helmets are highly recommended.

## Walking

All of Andalucía's towns and cities are highly walkable, and many areas are pedestrianized. On foot, you can take in the architectural details, absorb street life and peek into any church, shop or bar that catches your interest. Be aware that pavements can be narrow and uneven in historic centres. On hot days, try to keep to the shade and carry water with you at all times.

There are long-distance trails criss-crossing Andalucía for the more intrepid. One of the most established is the **GR7**, which starts at Tarifa and runs through Málaga and Granada, connecting the region with northern Spain, Andorra and France before linking, in Alsace, to the E5 path. In Granada's wild interior, the GR7 hops from village

to village. There is also a (chargeable) luggage transfer service which will pick up or drop off bags from the start or end of your planned walk.

The Camino Mozárabe is a waymarked route which serves as a conduit for pilgrims from south-eastern Spain as it is part of the famous St James Way network (known as the Camino de Santiago). The Andalucían section runs for 396 km (246 miles) from Granada to Córdoba and then to Mérida where it picks up the route north to Santiago de Compostela.

# Practical Information

## Passports and Visas

For entry requirements, including visas, consult your nearest Spanish embassy or check the **Exteriores** website. Visitors from outside the European Economic Area (EEA), European Union (EU) and Switzerland need a valid passport to enter Spain. EEA, EU and Swiss nationals can use identity cards instead.

From 2024, citizens of the UK, US, Canada, Australia and New Zealand do not need a visa for stays of up to three months, but must apply in advance for the European Travel Information and Authorization System (**ETIAS**). Visitors from other countries may also require an ETIAS, so check before travelling. EU nationals do not need a visa or an ETIAS. Schengen visas are valid for Spain.

A number of countries, including the UK, US, Canada and Ireland, have consulates in Andalucía and can provide consular assistance to nationals.

## Government Advice

Now more than ever, it is important to consult both your and the Spanish government's advice before travelling. The **UK Foreign & Commonwealth Office**, the **US Department of State**, the **Australian Department of Foreign Affairs and Trade** and the Spanish Exteriores website offer the latest information on security, health and local regulations.

## Customs Information

You can find information on the laws relating to goods and currency taken in or out of Andalucía and the Costa del Sol on the **Turespaña** (Spain's national tourist board) website.

For EU citizens there are no limits on most goods carried in or out of Spain as long as they are for personal use. There are, however, exceptions that include firearms and weapons, some types of food and plants and endangered species.

Non-EU citizens are allowed to import 200 cigarettes and a litre of spirits per adult, and can get a refund on Spain's 21 per cent sales tax (VAT, known here as IVA) on purchases over €90.15 – do this at the airport when leaving.

## Insurance

We recommend that you take out a comprehensive insurance policy covering theft, loss of belongings, medical care, cancellations and delays, and read the small print carefully.

UK citizens are eligible for free emergency medical care in Spain provided they have a valid European Health Insurance Card (**EHIC**) or UK Global Health Insurance Card (**GHIC**).

Spain has a reciprocal health agreement with other EU countries, and EU citizens receive emergency treatment under the public healthcare system if also carrying a valid EHIC. Prescriptions have to be paid for up-front. Non-EU visitors should check (with their embassy) to see if there are reciprocal arrangements with Spain.

## Health

Spain has a world-class healthcare system. Emergency medical care in Spain is free for all UK and EU citizens. If you have an EHIC or GHIC, be sure to present this as soon as possible. You may have to pay after treatment and reclaim the money later.

For visitors coming from outside the UK or EU, payment of medical expenses is the patient's responsibility, so it is important to arrange comprehensive insurance before travelling.

Seek medicinal supplies and advice for minor ailments from a pharmacy (farmacia), identifiable by a green or red cross. Each pharmacy displays a card in the window showing the address of the nearest all-night pharmacy, or call **Pharmacy on Duty** (or look online for Farmácias de Guardia) to locate the nearest one. Emergency contraception is available on prescription.

The cities and coastal areas of Andalucía have good hospitals and clinics. In an accident, or for urgent medical help, call the emergency services or the **Cruz Roja** (Red Cross), who will send an ambulance and paramedics. There are also dedicated lines for emergency dentists, narcotics or poisoning. If you are able to get to hospital, use the entrance marked *Urgencias* (Accident and Emergency). For less serious cases, visit one of the many private walk-in clinics. Consulates can provide a list of English-speaking physicians. Those covered by private health insurance can contact **Doctors on Call**.

For information regarding COVID-19 vaccination requirements, consult government advice. No other vaccinations are required to enter Spain, but routine vaccines should be kept up-to-date.

## Smoking, Alcohol and Drugs

Smoking is banned in enclosed public spaces and is a fineable offence, although you can still smoke on the terraces of bars and restaurants. Spain has a relaxed attitude towards alcohol consumption, but it is frowned upon to be visibly drunk.

The drink-drive limit is strictly enforced *(see p135)*. Recreational drugs are illegal, and possession of even a very small quantity can lead to an extremely hefty fine. Amounts that suggest an intent to supply drugs to other people can lead to custodial sentences.

## ID

By law you must carry identification with you at all times in Spain. A photocopy of your passport should suffice, but you may be asked to report to a police station with the original document. Keep your original passport safely stored in your hotel.

## Personal Security

Andalucía is a safe region to visit but petty crime does take place. Pickpockets work in known tourist areas, stations and busy streets. Use your common sense and be alert to your surroundings, and you should enjoy a stress-free trip.

If you do have anything stolen, report the crime within 24 hours to the nearest police station and take ID with you. Get a copy of the crime report *(denuncia)* to make an insurance claim. Contact your embassy if you have your passport stolen, or in the event of a serious crime.

As a rule, Andalucíans are very accepting of all people, regardless of their race, gender or sexuality. Homosexuality was legalized in Spain in 1979 and in 2007, the government recognized same-sex marriage and adoption rights for same-sex couples. That being said, the Catholic church still holds a lot of sway here and some conservative attitudes prevail, especially outside of urban areas. If you do feel unsafe, head for the nearest police station.

Torremolinos is a major centre for gay nightlife *(see p110)*. Seville, Granada and Cádiz also have thriving LGBTQ+ scenes.

Should you need them, Spain's **ambulance**, **police**, **fire** and **municipal police** services can be called for free from any landline, mobile or phone booth during a crisis.

## DIRECTORY

**PASSPORTS AND VISAS**

**ETIAS**
w etiasvisa.com

**Exteriores**
w exteriores.gob.es

**GOVERNMENT ADVICE**

**Australian Department of Foreign Affairs and Trade**
w smartraveller.gov.au

**UK Foreign & Commonwealth Office**
w gov.uk/foreign-travel-advice

**US State Department**
w travel.state.gov

**CUSTOMS INFORMATION**

**Turespaña**
w spain.info

**INSURANCE**

**EHIC**
w ec.europa.eu

**GHIC**
w ghic.org.uk

**HEALTH**

**Cruz Roja (Red Cross)**
( 952 22 22 22

**Doctors on Call**
( 112

**Pharmacy on Duty**
w farmacias.es

**PERSONAL SECURITY**

**Ambulance**
( 061 or 112

**Fire**
( 080 or 112

**Police**
( 091 or 112

**Municipal Police**
( 092

## Travellers with Specific Requirements

Spain is well-equipped when it comes to accessibility, but it is still advisable to call hotels and restaurants ahead of time and ask about the specific amenities available. The Confederación Española de Personas con Discapacidad Física y Orgánica (**COCEMFE**) and **Accessible Spain** provide information and tailored itineraries for those with reduced mobility, sight and hearing.

Spain's public transport system generally caters for all passengers, providing wheelchairs, adapted toilets and ramps. All public transport in Seville can accommodate wheelchair users. Airports offer reserved car parking, as well as other facilities. Metro maps in Braille are available from the Organización Nacional de Ciegos (**ONCE**).

## Time Zone

Spain is on Central European Time (CET), an hour ahead of Greenwich Mean Time, 6 hours ahead of US Eastern Standard Time and 11 hours behind Australian Eastern Standard Time. The clock moves forward 1 hour during daylight saving time from the last Sunday in March until the last Sunday in October.

## Money

Spain uses the euro (€). Most establishments accept major credit, debit and prepaid currency cards. Contactless payments are common in cities, but it's always a good idea to carry cash for smaller items and to buy transport tickets. ATMs are widely available throughout Andalucía, although many charge for cash withdrawals.

Spain does not have a big tipping culture, but it's appreciated and common to round-up the bill.

## Electrical Appliances

Power sockets are type F and C, fitting a two-prong, round-pin plug. Standard voltage is 230 volts.

## Mobile Phones and Wi-Fi

Cities and towns across Andalucía are provided with plenty of wireless internet hotspots. Visit the **WiFi Map** website to find free hotspots near you.

Visitors with EU tariffs can use their devices without being affected by roaming charges. Some UK networks have reintroduced roaming charges; check with your provider before travelling.

## Postal Services

Spanish mail is efficient, reliable and fast. **Correos**, is the national mail service; note that opening hours vary. Buy stamps from the post office or vending machines.

## Weather

The mild, Mediterranean climate in Andalucía is the envy of much of Europe. The year-round average temperature is 18–20° C (64–68° F) with 320 sunny days. Coastal areas have highs fluctuating between 15° C (59° F) and 30° C (86° F). Inland, average city highs vary from 12° C (54° F) in January to 36° C (97° F) in August.

Along the Costa del Sol it is mild and dry from April to September, very hot in July and August, and cool and wet in winter. Inland the temperature climbs where the wind is absent and falls where the land rises significantly, as in the Sierra Nevada and Alpujarra.

Every season offers its reasons to come here: summer for nightlife, spring and autumn for nature, winter for skiing. But autumn is arguably the best time – the weather and water are still warm, the crowds have gone, prices are lower and there are lots of local festivals.

## Opening Hours

Typical business hours are Monday–Saturday, 9:30am–1:30pm and 4:30–8pm. Major shopping centres and department stores are open all day 10am–9pm. In the high season in coastal areas many stay open until after 10pm. Smaller stores usually close by 3pm on Saturday.

Situations can change quickly and unexpectedly. Always check before visiting attractions and hospitality venues for up-to-date opening hours and booking requirements.

## Visitor Information

There are official tourist information booths at the airport and in cities and bigger towns. Here you can get maps and city passes that allow discounts on sights, arrange hop on/hop off bus tours, or find out what's on locally. The official websites for the **Andalucía** and **España** tourism boards offer further information.

Some cities offer a visitor's pass or discount card that can be used for free or reduced-price entry to events and museums, and even discounts at participating restaurants. Passes are not free, so consider carefully how many of the offers you are likely to take advantage of before purchasing one of them.

## Responsible Tourism

The climate crisis is having a big impact on Andalucía and the Costa del Sol, with droughts and heatwaves becoming more frequent. Do your bit by taking quick showers and reusing towels if staying in hotel accommodation. Andalucía is also at risk of wildfires so be careful when disposing of cigarette butts and glass bottles; starting a fire, even if accidental, is deemed a criminal offence.

## Bullfighting

*Corridas* (bullfights) are widely held in Andalucía. Supporters argue that the bulls are bred for the industry and would be killed as calves were it not for bullfighting, while some charities say that it's cruel and organize protests throughout the country. If you do decide to attend a *corrida*, bear in mind that it's better to see a big-name matador because they are more likely to make a clean and quick kill. The audience will make their disapproval evident if they don't.

## Language

*Castellano* (Castilian) is Spain's primary language and is spoken in Andalucía. English is widely spoken in the cities and other tourist spots, but the same cannot always be said for rural areas. Mastering a few phrases in *Castellano* will go down well with locals.

## Taxes and Refunds

IVA (value added tax) in mainland Spain tends to be 21 per cent, but with lower rates for certain goods and services.

Under certain conditions, non-EU citizens can claim a rebate of these taxes. Retailers can give you a form to fill out, which you can then present to a customs officer at your point of departure. If the shop offers IVA, you can fill that form out instead and validate it at one of the self-service machines found at Spain's main ports and airports.

## Accommodation

Andalucía offers everything from boutique villas to campsites. Throughout peak season (June to August) and during major fiestas, room rates are high and hotels are soon fully booked, so reserve in advance where possible. Most hotels quote their prices without including tax, which is 10 per cent.

Sites such as **Trivago**, **Laterooms** and **Booking. com** can help you explore the range of options.

### DIRECTORY

**TRAVELLERS WITH SPECIFIC REQUIREMENTS**

**Accessible Spain**
w accessiblespain travel.com

**COCEMFE**
w cocemfe.es

**ONCE**
w once.es

**MOBILE PHONES AND WI-FI**

**WiFi Map**
w wifimap.io

**POSTAL SERVICES**

**Correos**
w correos.es

**VISITOR INFORMATION**

**Andalucía**
w andalucia.org

**España**
w spain.info

**ACCOMMODATION**

**Booking.com**
w booking.com

**Laterooms**
w laterooms.com

**Trivago**
w trivago.com

# Places to Stay

## PRICE CATEGORIES

For a standard, double room per night (with breakfast if included), taxes and extra charges.

€ under €100    €€ €100–€200    €€€ over €200

## Seville Stays

### Hotel Un Patio al Sur
MAP L2 ■ C/Fernán Caballero 7 ■ 954 22 10 35 ■ www.patioalsur.es ■ €€
Housed in an 18th-century Andalucían mansion, this eco-friendly boutique hotel is conveniently located near the Museo de Bellas Artes. The rooftop terrace offers wonderful city views. Free Wi-Fi.

### Oasis Backpackers' Palace
MAP L2 ■ C/Almirante Ulloa 1 ■ 955 22 82 87 ■ www.oasisseville. com ■ €
Once a grand palace, this hostel has spacious dorms and double rooms with en-suite bathrooms. There's free Wi-Fi, a shared kitchen, lounge and rooftop pool.

### Alcoba del Rey
MAP N1 ■ C/Becquer 9 ■ 954 91 58 00 ■ www. alcobadelrey.com ■ €€
This boutique hotel features Indian- and Moroccan-style decor and king-size canopy beds. Great views from the rooftop terrace. Free Wi-Fi.

### H10 Corregidor Boutique Hotel
MAP M1 ■ C/Morgado 17 ■ 954 38 51 11 ■ www. h10hotels.com ■ €€€
This comfortable boutique hotel is just around the corner from the lively Alameda de Hercules in a trendy part of town. It provides a rooftop plunge pool and free access to a gym across the street. Free Wi-Fi.

### Murillo Apartamentos
MAP M4 ■ Lope de Rueda 16 ■ 954 21 60 95 ■ www. hotelmurillo.com ■ €€
These lovely apartments are named after the Baroque painter who hailed from the flower-decked old quarter, where they are located. The terrace offers great city views. Free Wi-Fi.

### EME Catedral Mercer Hotel
MAP M3 ■ C/Alemanes 27 ■ 954 56 00 00 ■ www. emecatedralmercer.com ■ €€€
Opposite the cathedral, this hotel has a trendy ambience. Highlights include a spa, a gym, an excellent Italian restaurant, a Mediterranean-fusion bistro and a rooftop lounge with unparalleled views.

### Eurostars Sevilla Boutique
MAP M2 ■ C/Abades 41 ■ 954 97 90 09 ■ www. eurostarshotels.com ■ €€€
In the heart of Barrio de Santa Cruz, with excellent views of the Giralda and the cathedral from its roof terrace, expect minimalist luxury in contrast to the classic façade. There's an outdoor pool.

### Hotel Alfonso XIII
MAP M4 ■ C/San Fernando 2 ■ 954 91 70 00 ■ www.mariott.com ■ €€€
This historic palace, now a five-star hotel, was erected by the eponymous king to house royals and other dignitaries during the 1929 Exposition. Rooms are luxuriously decorated, and the hotel has an outdoor swimming pool with alfresco dining alongside.

### La Parada del Marqués
MAP K2 ■ C/Zaragoza 20 ■ 954 50 27 21 ■ €€€
A charming boutique hotel, with a rooftop terrace, which blends historical architectural features with contemporary furniture and upcycled wooden doors. It is close to the Plaza de Armas bus station, the shopping district and the Museo de Bellas Artes

### Las Casas del Rey de Baeza
MAP N2 ■ Plaza Jesús de la Redención 2 ■ 954 56 14 96 ■ www.hospes.es ■ €€€
Close to La Casa de Pilatos, this chic hotel is located in a beautiful setting, which fuses historic traditional architecture with modern style. Shaded walkways and stone flooring echo the natural tones in the courtyards. The rooftop pool is a bonus.

### Melía Colón Hotel
MAP L2 ■ C/Canalejas 1 ■ 954 50 55 99 ■ www. melia.com ■ €€€
This grand five-star hotel combines Andalucían elegance and maximum

comfort. Enjoy fabulous views from the solarium, cool off in the pool or relax in the spa. The cocktail bar hosts live music.

## Granada Stays

### Hotel Rosa D'Oro
MAP R2 ■ Carrera del Darro 23 ■ 958 21 57 30 ■ www.hotelrosadeoro.es ■ €€

A former Franciscan convent, this 16th-century palace overlooking the Darro River has been restored in its original style. Some of the rooms have spectacular views and there is also an elegant central courtyard.

### Hotel Sacromonte
MAP F4 ■ Plaza del Lino 1 ■ 958 26 64 11 ■ www. hotelsacromonte.es ■ €€

This modern, three-star hotel in the centre of Granada has beautifully appointed rooms, a well-equipped gym and a swimming pool for relaxing. Free WiFi.

### Hotelito Boutique Suecia
MAP R3 ■ C/Molinos (Huerta de los Angeles) 8 ■ 958 22 50 44 ■ €

In a leafy cul-de-sac, this traditional Andalucían house has arched windows, terracotta tiles and a patio. The rooftop terrace is perfect for admiring the nearby Alhambra. Free Wi-Fi.

### Oasis Backpackers' Hostel
MAP Q2 ■ Placeta Correo Viejo 3 ■ 958 21 58 48 ■ www.oasisgranada. com/granada-hostel ■ €

Set in a historic building, this hostel has a rooftop terrace with great views,

an interior patio, a bar, a kitchen and free Wi-Fi. All rooms are en-suite. The hostel also organizes activities for its guests to explore the city.

### Posada Pilar del Toro
MAP Q2 ■ C/Elvira 25 ■ 958 22 73 33 ■ www. posadadeltoro.com ■ €

In the heart of the Albaicín, this *posada* features traditional wooden beams and ceramic tiles, creating a rustic ambience with modern comforts.

### Palacete 1620 Premium Suites
MAP Q2 ■ Plaza de los Lobos 6 ■ 958 87 05 50 ■ www.palacete1620.com ■ €€

Set in a 17th-century manor house, these stately apartments have been meticulously designed, respecting original elements yet offering modern comfort and elegance. The apartments are arranged around an inner courtyard. Adults only.

### Gar Anat Hotel
MAP Q2 ■ Carrera del Darro 13 ■ 958 21 50 40 ■ www.ladrondeagua. com ■ €€

This superbly located boutique hotel is set in a 16th-century mansion. Eight of the beautifully decorated rooms have views of the Alhambra. Guests can enjoy complimentary appetizers and wines every evening.

### Hotel Reina Cristina
MAP F4 ■ C/Tablas 4 ■ 958 25 32 11 ■ www.hotel reinacristina.com ■ €€

Everything has been kept more or less the same as when the poet Garcia Lorca was forced to hide

out here – this is the last place the poet stayed, before his untimely end *(see p55)*. Each room has a unique style and there are patios and fountains in the public areas.

### Room Mate Leo
MAP Q3 ■ C/Mesones 15 ■ 958 53 55 79 ■ www. room-matehotels.com ■ €€

This trendy hotel is located on a pedestrianised street within walking distance of most sights. There are stunning views of the Alhambra and the city from the top floor terrace and some rooms, which are modern, with a creative mix of colour and decor. There's a breakfast buffet available until noon.

### Alhambra Palace
MAP R3 ■ Plaza Arquitecto García de Paredes 1 ■ 958 22 14 68 ■ www.h-alhambra palace.es ■ €€€

The style of this *belle époque* extravaganza is Neo-Moorish. The public rooms are palatial. Just steps away from the Nasrid palace, it has great views from every room, terrace and balcony.

## Paradors

### Parador Alcázar del Rey, Carmona
MAP C3 ■ Alcázar s/n ■ 954 14 10 10 ■ €€

One of the most impressive of all the paradors, this 14th-century Moorish fortress-palace overlooks the Río Corbones. Rooms are large and decorated in classic Andalucían style, set off by antiques. Cool off in the garden pool or on the expansive terrace.

### Parador Arcos de la Frontera
MAP C5 ▪ Plaza del Cabildo ▪ 956 70 05 00 ▪ €€

Right on the banks of the Río Guadalete, this has an impressive view of the fertile plain of the river and of the old part of town. An ideal starting point for the *pueblos blancos* routes, as well as Jerez de la Frontera. The courtyard is graced with traditional latticework and ceramic tiles.

### Parador Condestable Dávalos, Úbeda
MAP F2 ▪ Plaza de Vázquez Molina ▪ 953 75 03 45 ▪ €€

Live like 16th-century nobility in a Renaissance palace in the heart of one of Spain's best preserved historic centres. Rooms reflect the noble tone, with high ceilings and antique furnishings.

### Parador de Antequera
MAP D4 ▪ Paseo García del Olmo 2 ▪ 952 84 02 61 ▪ €€

This quiet parador, surrounded by gardens and a swimming pool, is near the spectacular El Torcal (see p61). The rooms offer scenic views of the Andalucían landscape.

### Parador de Ayamonte
MAP A4 ▪ Avda de la Constitucíon ▪ 959 32 07 00 ▪ €€

A modern facility with sunlit rooms and a perfect position for exploring the area where Huelva Province meets Portugal. Most rooms afford panoramic views of the Atlantic from the high point of town.

### Parador de Cazorla
MAP G3 ▪ 953 72 70 75 ▪ Sierra de Cazorla s/n ▪ Closed Jan–Feb ▪ €€

In a remote location in the heart of the Parque Natural Sierra de Cazorla, with stunning views, this graceful country house lets you relax in comfort. The restaurant offers regional fare and game in season.

### Parador de Ronda
MAP D5 ▪ Plaza de España ▪ 952 87 75 00 ▪ €€€

Set in the former town hall, views from the rooms are amazing, while the decor reflects the colours of the area.

### Parador del Gilbralfaro, Málaga
MAP S4 ▪ Castillo de Gibralfaro ▪ 952 22 19 02 ▪ €€€

Facing the Alcázaba this parador stands surrounded by pine trees. It's handy for golf courses and tennis nearby.

### Parador de Mazagón
MAP B4 ▪ Ctra San Juan del Puerto-Matalascañas km 31 ▪ 959 53 63 00 ▪ €€€

Unspoiled beauty on the shores of the sea is what this modern property is all about. It's ideal for those who want to commune with nature, especially with the wonders of the Coto Doñana nearby. Facilities include gardens, pools and a sauna – all facing Mazagón beach.

### Parador de Mójacar
MAP H4 ▪ Paseo del Mediterraneo 339 ▪ 950 47 82 50 ▪ €€€

This beachside parador, 1.5 km (1 mile) from the village of Mójacar and 3 km (just under 2 miles) from a golf course, has an inviting atmosphere with spectacular views from the bedroom terraces and the upstairs dining room. Ultra-modern, clean and child-friendly.

### Parador de San Francisco, Granada
MAP S3 ▪ C/Real de la Alhambra ▪ 958 22 14 40 ▪ €€€

You'll need to book about a year in advance to lodge here, but it's the premier stay in town. Housed in a restored 15th-century monastery, with a wisteria-covered patio, it is truly beautiful. For the best experience, get a room with a view out over the Albaicín on one side and the cloister on the other.

## Luxury Hotels

### Casa Vesta, Zufre
MAP B3 ▪ C/Santa Zita, Zufre ▪ 647 72 38 08 ▪ www.casa-vesta.com ▪ €€

Located in the countryside of Huelva, this charming boutique hotel has world-class service. There's a billiards room, library, outdoor swimming pool and free Wi-Fi. No under-16s.

### Hotel Infanta Cristina, Jaen
MAP E3 ▪ Avenida de Madrid 1 ▪ 953 26 30 40 ▪ www.hotelinfanta cristina.com ▪ €€€

Located in the heart of Jaen, this contemporary hotel offers tastefully decorated rooms and suites. The restaurant offers traditional delicacies. There is an outdoor pool and a solarium.

### Hotel Jerez & Spa, Jerez
MAP B5 ▪ Avda Álvaro Domecq 35 ▪ 956 30 06 00 ▪ www.hace.es ▪ €€
Rooms here have been decorated in a warm style and overlook the gardens. All have satellite TV and Internet; many also have a Jacuzzi. There's a delightful spa.

### Hotel Montelirio, Ronda
MAP D5 ▪ C/Tenorio 8 ▪ 952 87 38 55 ▪ www. hotelmontelirio.com ▪ €€
A beautifully restored 17th-century palace offering every comfort. Perched on the edge of Ronda's famous gorge, it has stunning views. There's an outdoor pool and a Turkish bath.

### Club Marítimo de Sotogrande
MAP C6 ▪ Puerto Deportivo, Sotogrande ▪ 956 79 02 00 ▪ www. clubmaritimodesoto grande.com ▪ €€€
Luxurious and tastefully decorated in neutral tones, this hotel affords amazing views from every room – sometimes from the bathtub. Free bike use and discounts for golfing.

### El Fuerte, Marbella
MAP D5 ▪ Avda El Fuerte ▪ 952 86 15 00 ▪ www. fuertehoteles.com ▪ €€€
In the centre of Marbella, this hotel is next to the sea and surrounded by subtropical gardens. It is within easy walking distance of the historic quarter too, so you can discover the "real" Marbella, as well as soak up the glamour. Minimum two- or three-night stay during peak seasons.

### Hospes Palacio del Bailío, Córdoba
MAP D3 ▪ Ramírez de las Casas Deza 10–12 ▪ 957 49 89 93 ▪ www.hospes. es ▪ €€€
Dating back to the 16th century, Hospes Palacio del Bailío is a complex of former granaries, coach houses and stables surrounded by beautiful gardens and patios.

### Hotel Barrosa Palace, Chiclana de la Frontera
MAP B5 ▪ Novo Sancti Petri ▪ 956 49 22 00 ▪ www.hipotels.com/ hotel-barrosa-palace-en-cadiz.htm ▪ €€
A spa-resort right on the beach, just south of Cádiz. It has three restaurants, a fitness centre, indoor and outdoor pools and a range of beauty treatments. Minimum two- or three-night stay during high seasons.

### Vincci Selección Aleysa, Benalmádena
MAP D5 ▪ Avda Antonio Machado 57 ▪ 952 56 65 66 ▪ www.vinccihoteles. com ▪ €€€
This boutique hotel on the beachfront has great sea views. There's a wellness spa and healthy activities including free yoga and pilates in the garden.

## Resorts

### Barceló Jerez, Montecastillo
MAP B5 ▪ Ctra Jerez-Arcos km 6 ▪ 956 15 12 040 ▪ www.hotelbarcelo montecastillo.com ▪ €€
Towering like a castle of pale yellow stucco beside one of Europe's top golf courses, the hotel gives lots of activity, eating and drinking options.

### Hotel Paraíso del Mar, Nerja
MAP E5 ▪ C/Prolongación de Carabeo 22 ▪ 952 52 16 21 ▪ www.hotel paraisodelmar.es ▪ €€
All rooms at this converted villa have a Jacuzzi and a terrace with views of either the beach, the mountains or the hotel's gardens. Guests have private access to the Burriana beach.

### Hotel Playa de la Luz, Rota
MAP B5 ▪ Avda de la Diputación ▪ 956 81 05 00 ▪ www.hace.es/en/ hotelplayadelaluz ▪ €€
Most rooms have a terrace or balcony at this hotel, nestled by an unspoiled beach. Minimum two- or three-night stay during peak seasons.

### Hotel Vincci Rumaykiyya, Sierra Nevada, Monachil
MAP F4 ▪ Urb. Sol y Nieve s/n ▪ 958 48 25 08 ▪ www. vinccihoteles.com ▪ Closed mid-Apr–Dec ▪ €€
With an alpine-style decor, Hotel Vincci Rumaykiyya is at the heart of the ski resort. The terrace offers great views of the surrounding.

### Tui Blue Isla Cristina Palace & Spa, Isla Cristina
MAP A4 ▪ Avda del Parque s/n ▪ 959 34 44 99 ▪ www.tuiblueisla cristinapalace.com ▪ €€
Enjoy beachfront access and a range of massages, Turkish baths and saunas. All rooms have balconies.

*For a key to hotel price categories see p140*

### Barceló la Bobadilla, Loja (Granada)

MAP E4 ▪ Ctra Salinas-Villanueva de Tapia (A333) km 65.5 ▪ 958 32 18 61 ▪ www.barcelo.com ▪ €€€

Fabulous and reminiscent of a tiny Moorish village with its own chapel, Barceló la Bobadilla features beautiful gardens and charming patios.

### Hotel Fuerte Conil, Conil de la Frontera

MAP B5 ▪ Playa de la Fontanilla ▪ 956 44 33 44 ▪ www.fuerte-hoteles.com ▪ Closed Nov–Feb ▪ €€€

An award-winner for its environmentally friendly practices, this Neo-Moorish-style resort is not far from the fishing village of Conil. There's a choice of rest-aurants, a pool, spa and sports facilities.

### Hotel La Fuente de la Higuera, Ronda

MAP D5 ▪ Partido de los Frontones ▪ 952 16 56 08 ▪ www.hotel-lafuente.com ▪ €€€

Set in a renovated olive oil mill where Spanish architecture meets Post-Modern design. Rooms have individually designed interiors and a garden area or terrace. There's also an outdoor pool.

### Kempinski Resort Hotel, Estepona

MAP D5 ▪ Ctra de Cádiz km 159 ▪ 952 80 95 00 ▪ www.kempinski.com/es/marbella ▪ €€€

A magnificent resort with a whimsical take on Moorish and regional architecture that suits the seaside setting perfectly.

### Marriott Marbella Beach Resort

MAP D5 ▪ Marbella del Este, Ctra de Cádiz km 193 ▪ 952 76 96 00 ▪ www.marriott.com ▪ €€€

Surrounded by lush gardens with multiple pools, a great gym, sauna and plenty of activities to keep children amused.

## Historic Finds

### Hotel La Casa del Califa, Vejer de la Frontera

MAP C6 ▪ Plaza de España 16 ▪ 956 44 77 30 ▪ www.califavejer.com ▪ €€

A sojourn at this hotel, created out of eight different houses including the 17th-century Casa del Juzgado, is like staying in a private house. Excellent views and service and a recommended restaurant.

### Palacio de la Rambla, Úbeda

MAP F2 ▪ Plaza del Marqués 1 ▪ 953 75 01 96 ▪ www.palaciodela rambla.com ▪ €€

This 16th-century palace offers eight rooms for guests to experience the refined atmosphere. The patio is said to have been designed by the architect Andrés de Vandelvira.

### Amanhavis Hotel, Benahavis, Málaga

MAP D5 ▪ C/Pilar 3 ▪ 952 85 60 26 ▪ www.amanhavis.com ▪ Closed mid-Jan–mid-Feb ▪ €€

This place is like an Andalucían theme park, albeit very tasteful. Rooms are linked to an episode in Spanish history, such as Boabdil or Christopher Columbus, and styled accordingly. Free Wi-Fi.

### Hacienda de Orán, Utrera

MAP C4 ▪ Ctra A8029 km 7 ▪ 955 81 59 94 ▪ www.haciendadeoran.com ▪ €€

This stately 17th-century Andalucían manor is decorated with antiques and rich textiles. There are bougainvillea-covered porches, horse stables, a carriage museum, a pool and even a small airstrip.

### Hotel Convento Aracena

MAP B3 ▪ C/Jesus y Maria 19 ▪ 959 12 68 99 ▪ www.hotelconvento aracena.es ▪ €€

Housed in a 17th-century convent, this hotel has an outdoor pool as well as a spa and wellness centre. Buffet breakfast. Bike hire available at the reception.

### Hotel Hacienda Posada de Vallina, Córdoba

MAP D3 ▪ C/Corregidor Luis de la Cerda 83 ▪ 957 49 87 50 ▪ www.hhposa dadevallina.es ▪ €€

In the heart of Córdoba's Jewish Quarter, this charming, historic hotel retains original features, including beamed ceilings and exposed stone walls.

### Crisol Monasterio de San Miguel, El Puerto de Santa María

MAP B5 ▪ C/Virgen de los Milagros 27 ▪ 956 54 04 40 ▪ www.monasteriosan miguelhotel.com ▪ €€

This former monastery, with Baroque architecture and art, is equipped with modern luxuries including an excellent restaurant, a pool and a solarium.

### Hotel Puerta de la Luna, Baeza
MAP F2 ▪ Canónigo Melgares Raya s/n ▪ 953 74 70 19 ▪ www.hotel puertadelaluna.com ▪ €€
Set in a 16th-century building, Hotel Puerta de la Luna is in the heart of old Baeza. Rooms are each uniquely furnished. Free Wi-Fi and an outdoor pool.

### Soho Boutique Palacio San Gabriel, Ronda
MAP D5 ▪ C/Marqués de Moctezuma 19 ▪ 952 19 03 92 ▪ www. en.sohohoteles.com ▪ Closed 1–9 Jan, 19–31 Jul & 21–31 Dec ▪ €€
Built in 1736, this converted mansion, with its original coat of arms and handsome façade, offers sumptuous rooms for the price.

### NH Amistad Córdoba
MAP D3 ▪ Plaza de Maimónides 3 ▪ 957 42 03 35 ▪ www.nh-hotels. com ▪ €€€
Just a few minutes from La Mezquita and built into the old city walls. The large patio-cloisters are lovely, and there's also a plunge pool and sun terrace. Free Wi-Fi.

## Budget Charmers

### Hosteria Lineros 38, Córdoba
MAP D3 ▪ C/Lineros 38 ▪ 957 48 25 17 ▪ www. hotelriadlineros38. mydirectstay.com ▪ €€
With its striking Mudéjar-style architecture, Hosteria Lineros 38 is a pleasing building that epitomizes the city's cross-cultural charm. It's a great choice in the old quarter. Free Wi-Fi.

### Hotel Doña Blanca, Jerez de la Frontera
MAP B5 ▪ C/Bodegas 11 ▪ 956 34 87 61 ▪ www. hoteldonablanca.com ▪ €
This place provides all the services you'd expect of more high-end properties. The rooms are maintained well, and there's parking and free Wi-Fi.

### Hotel Embarcadero de Calahonda de Granada
MAP F5 ▪ C/Biznaga 14 ▪ 958 62 30 11 ▪ www. embarcaderodecala honda.com ▪ €
Set right on the beach, this hotel has stylish, well-equipped rooms overlooking the sea.

### Hotel González, Córdoba
MAP D3 ▪ C/Manríquez 3 ▪ 957 47 98 19 ▪ www. hotel-gonzalez.com ▪ €€
This charming hotel typifies the old houses of the Jewish Quarter, with a central patio and an elegant marble entrance replete with antiques and high ceilings. Free Wi-Fi.

### Hotel Palacio de Hemingway
MAP D5 ▪ C/Tenorio 1, Ronda ▪ 952 87 01 01 ▪ €
This elegant mansion was once the home of the poet Pedro Pérez Clotet. The 12 rooms house hand-made Andalucían-style furniture. The terrace-restaurant offers great city views. Free Wi-Fi.

### La Casa Campana, Arcos de la Frontera
MAP C5 ▪ Nuñez de Prado 4 ▪ 600 28 49 28 ▪ www.casacampana. com ▪ €
This hotel features seven en-suite rooms (one of them an apartment) and

a terrace offering city and river views. Breakfast is not included in the price of stay. Free Wi-Fi.

### La Casa Grande, Arcos de la Frontera
MAP C5 ▪ C/Maldonado 10 ▪ 956 70 39 30 ▪ www. lacasagrande.net ▪ Closed 6 Jan–6 Feb ▪ €
In 1729, the Nuñez de Prado family erected this mansion. Perched over the cliff of La Peña, it features ceramic tiles, stone columns, wood beams and antiques. Free Wi-Fi.

### Pensión Sevillano, Nerja
MAP E5 ▪ C/Almirante Ferrandiz 31 ▪ 952 52 15 23 ▪ www.pension sevillano.com ▪ €
A family-run hostel in the heart of Nerja, it is taste-fully decorated with a Moroccan theme. Rooms are comfortable and have ceiling fans, fridges and are en-suite. There is a delightful roof terrace.

### Hotel Argantonio, Cádiz
MAP B5 ▪ C/Argantonio 3, Cádiz ▪ 956 21 16 40 ▪ www.hotelargantonio. es ▪ €
Located in the old town, each floor of this hotel is decorated with a different theme. All rooms have a bath, a flat-screen TV and free Wi-Fi. Some rooms have balconies.

### Hotel TRH, Baeza
MAP F2 ▪ C/Concepción 3 ▪ 953 74 81 30 ▪ www. trhbaeza.com ▪ €
Right in the heart of this Renaissance town is this oasis of quiet beauty. It's part of a chain, with all the conveniences, yet evokes timeless style.

*For a key to hotel price categories see p140*

# Rural Retreats

## Alcázar de la Reina, Carmona
MAP C3 ▪ Hermana Concepción Orellana 2 ▪ 954 19 62 00 ▪ www.alcazar-reina.es ▪ €

In the historic centre of this small town, the façade of this hotel stands out, while the interior reflects Mudéjar craftsmanship. No two rooms are alike, but they all have marble bathrooms and many offer spectacular views.

## Alquería de los Lentos, Niguelas
MAP F4 ▪ Camino de los Molinos ▪ 659 91 29 61 ▪ www.alqueriadeloslentos.com ▪ €

Surrounded by orchards at the foothills of the Sierra Nevada, this 16th-century mill has been lovingly transformed into a small hotel and organic restaurant. There is a swimming pool, and most rooms have terraces.

## Antonio, Zahara de los Atunes
MAP C6 ▪ Atlanterra km 1 ▪ 956 43 91 41 ▪ www.antoniohoteles.com ▪ €€

This seaside retreat is decorated in a traditional style, with whitewashed walls, and there's a nice pool. Most rooms have terraces with sea views.

## Casa Don Carlos, Alhaurin el Grande
MAP D5 ▪ Ctra Coin Churriana km 3.5, Alhaurin el Grande ▪ 669 94 50 46 ▪ www.casadoncarlos.com ▪ €

This award-winning, adults only bed and breakfast, facing Alhaurin el Grande, has magnificent views of the countryside.

The rooms are clean and comfortable. Guests can hire cars and motorcycles.

## Casas Cuevas La Tala, near Guadix
MAP F4 ▪ A-92N km 1.5, Camino de La Tala al Perro ▪ 958 66 29 54 ▪ www.casascuevalatala.com ▪ €

A complex of stylishly preserved cave dwellings and an 18th-century manor house, some with hydro-massage tubs. Outdoor pool, barbecue and lovely grounds provide the perfect setting for relaxation.

## Casona de Calderón Hotel, Osuna
MAP D4 ▪ Plaza Cervantes 16 ▪ 954 81 50 37 ▪ www.casonacalderon.es ▪ €

Set in a historic town near Seville, this exquisite boutique hotel offers a calming ambience. Along with rooms that feature a vintage flair and antique-style decorations, there's a lovely patio with an outdoor pool and an excellent restaurant.

## Hotel Villa Maria, Cabra
MAP E3 ▪ C/Antonio Povedano 23 ▪ 857 89 40 40 ▪ www.villamariacabra.com ▪ €

Set on the edge of the Subbética mountain range, this restored manor house offers 12 beautifully furnished rooms. The on-site restaurant can prepare picnic lunches.

## Cortijo El Sotillo, San José
MAP H5 ▪ Ctra Entrada a San José ▪ 950 61 11 00 ▪ www.playasycortijos.com ▪ €€

A tranquil base from which to explore the beaches of

Cabo de Gata. The rooms here are spacious and have large terraces with beautiful views.

## Finca Buen Vino, Sierra de Aracena
MAP B3 ▪ Los Marines, N433 km 95 ▪ 959 12 40 34 ▪ www.fincabuenvino.com ▪ €€

A converted ranch, set amid green hills, this bed and breakfast is filled with an eclectic mix of furniture, paintings, pottery and books. Rooms are all distinctive, and there are self-catering cottages with a private pool available, too. Check the website for special activities.

## La Almendra y el Gitano, Agua Amarga
MAP G4 ▪ Camino Cala del Plomo, Agua Amarga ▪ 678 50 29 11 ▪ www.laalmendrayelgitano.com ▪ €€€

In the heart of a natural park, close to unspoiled beaches, and with no phones or Internet, this is a haven of tranquillity. There's a community kitchen for guests' use.

# Hostels, Camping and Self-Catered

## Albergue Inturjoven, Marbella
MAP D5 ▪ C/Trapiche 2 ▪ 955 18 11 81 ▪ www.inturjoven.com ▪ €

Shared dorms, double rooms, a pool and recreational options make this an excellent youth hostel. It's just north of Casco Antiguo (old quarter), where you can see the real Marbella. Walk through its narrow, cobbled streets to get to the beach and the port.

### Camping Cabo de Gata, Cabo de Gata
MAP H5 ■ Ctra Cabo de Gata, Cortijo Ferrón ■ 950 16 04 43 ■ www.campingcabodegata.com ■ €

This campsite offers shady areas for tents, trailers and RV hook-ups, as well as bungalows. Facilities include a pool, access to pristine beaches and a reception centre with safes.

### Camping Conil, Conil de la Frontera
MAP B5 ■ Carril Hijuela de la Mirla 86 ■ 956 92 24 18 ■ www.camping conil.es ■ €

Set in a tranquil pine forest close to the coast, this campsite features a swimming pool, tennis courts, a mini-mart, bar, restaurant and laundry facilities.

### Camping El Sur, Ronda
MAP D5 ■ Ctra Ronda-Algeciras km 1.5 ■ 952 87 59 39 ■ www.camping elsur.com ■ €

Camping and bungalows with kitchen and bathroom are available here. It's a chance to take beautiful walks or horse ride in the countryside around Ronda.

### Hostal la Fuente, Córdoba
MAP D3 ■ C/San Fernando 51 ■ 957 48 78 27 ■ www.hostal lafuente.com ■ €

A charming budget hotel in the centre of Córdoba, offering single, double, triple and quadruple rooms as well as some apartments. There's a rooftop terrace with an adjoining café, a central courtyard and a large communal lounge.

### Hostal La Malagueña, Estepona
MAP D5 ■ C/Raphael 1 ■ 952 80 00 11 ■ www.hlmestepona.com ■ €

Although it isn't an official hostel or even aimed at backpackers, the price doesn't get any better than this. The airy rooms have balconies facing the square. You can stroll along the sandy beaches or wander around the shops of this old fishing village.

### Hostal La Posada, Mijas
MAP D5 ■ C/Coin 47 & 49 ■ 952 48 53 10 ■ €

Rent a fully equipped apartment in this white village and sample a bit of the real Andalucía. Not all have air conditioning.

### Instalación Juvenil, Sol y Nieve, Sierra Nevada
MAP F4 ■ C/Peñones 22 ■ 955 18 11 81 ■ www.inturjoven.com ■ €

Located near the top of the ski station, with rooms holding two to six, this place is ideal for skiers in the winter or trekkers during summer. Skis and other equipment for hire.

### Los Castillarejos Apartamentos Rurales, Luque
MAP D3 ■ Ctra CO-6203 km 5.7, Luque ■ 957 09 00 12 ■ www.loscastillarejos.com ■ €

A set of 14 modern apartments decorated using natural materials and local stone. Kitchens are fully equipped; there's a pool and free Wi-Fi.

### Cantueso, Periana
MAP E4 ■ Periana, Málaga ■ 699 94 62 13 ■ www.cantueso.net ■ €€

Ten whitewashed cottages with private terraces enjoy a splendid mountainside setting. Lush gardens provide tranquillity. Not all have air conditioning.

### Casas Karen, Costa de la Luz
MAP C6 ■ Camino del Monte 6, nr Cabo Trafalgar ■ 956 43 70 67 ■ www.casaskaren.com ■ €€

Typical Andalucían *chozas* (traditional, thatched straw bungalows) and converted farm buildings between pine woods and the beach. Follow signs to Faro de Trafalgar.

### Casas Rurales Benarum, Mecina Bombarón
MAP F4 ■ C/Casas Blancas 1 ■ 958 85 11 49 ■ www.benarum.com ■ €

Twelve rural cabins, each accommodating two to five people, nestle in this quiet mountain town. The cabins are fully equipped and there is a pool and spa on site.

### Torre de la Peña, Tarifa
MAP C6 ■ Ctra N340, Tarifa ■ 956 68 49 03 ■ www.campingtp.com ■ €

This lovely site offers beachfront camping and bungalows, with spectacular views. It is perfect for watersports such as windsurfing, kitesurfing and snorkelling. There's a good restaurant on site serving Spanish cuisine made from fresh, locally produced ingredients.

*For a key to hotel price categories see p140*

# General Index

# Acknowledgments

## This edition updated by

**Contributor** Lynnette McCurdy Bastida

**Senior Editors** Dipika Dasgupta, Alison McGill

**Senior Art Editor** Stuti Tiwari

**Project Editor** Sarah Allen

**Art Editor** Bineet Kaur

**Picture Research Administrator** Vagisha Pushp

**Picture Research Manager** Taiyaba Khatoon

**Publishing Assistant** Simona Velikova

**Jacket Designer** Jordan Lambley

**Senior Cartographer** Subhashree Bharati

**Cartography Manager** Suresh Kumar

**Senior DTP Designer** Tanveer Zaidi

**Senior Production Editor** Jason Little

**Production Controller** Kariss Ainsworth

**Managing Editors** Shikha Kulkarni, Beverly Smart, Hollie Teague

**Managing Art Editor** Sarah Snelling

**Senior Managing Art Editor** Priyanka Thakur

**Art Director** Maxine Pedliham

**Publishing Director** Georgina Dee

DK would like to thank the following for their contribution to the previous editions: Kathryn Glendenning, Jeffrey Kennedy, Chris Moss, Helen Peters

The publisher would like to thank the following for their kind permission to reproduce their photographs:

**Key:** a-above; b-below/bottom; c-centre; f-far; l-left; r-right; t-top

**Alamy Stock Photo:** a-plus image bank 15bl, 81tr; age fotostock/Alberto Paredes 128tl, / Alvaro Leiva 71crb, /Francisco Barba 26br, / Rafael Campillo 73cl, /J.D. Dallet 122cl, /Juan José Pascual 57cr, 125tr; age fotostock 76cl; Guillermo Aguilar 14bl; Jerónimo Alba 54cr, 62-3, 79clb, 80b; Album/Francesc Fàbregas 51clb; Peter Barritt 48cl; Artur Bogacki 65cl; Tibor Bognar 11cr, 34bl; Bon Appetit/ FoodPhotogr. Eising 77tr; Charles Bowman 64tl; Michelle Chaplow 72br; CHROMORANGE/ Günter Fischer 67tr; Classic Image 52cra; classicpaintings 48tr; Stuart Crump HDR 69tr; colau 50bl; Design Pics Inc/Ken Welsh 44tc; Ilja Dubovskis 99cb; Hemis.fr/Bruno Morandi 46t, /Bertrand Reiger 22crb; Heritage Image Partnership Ltd/ Werner Forman Archive 45c; Peter Horree 108cla; Jam World Images 56cl, 61tr, 98b; John Kellerman 18bl, 87cl; LOOK Die Bildagentur der Fotografen GmbH/Ingolf Pompe 110bl; Jose Lucas 47cl; Clement McCarthy 46bl; Angus McComiskey 7t; Tim Moore 128bc; Hilary Morgan 55crb; Perry van Munster 101cr, 113clb; myLAM 129cr; Peter Netley 39clb; Sean Pavone 22-3; philipus 95tl; Ingolf Pompe 87 112tl; QED images 48bc; Rolf Richardson 49clb; Robertharding / Frank Fell 3tr, 130-131; Robert Harding Productions 47tr; Rolf Hicker Photography 58br, 116tr; Pascal Saez 38-9, 80cla; Scott Rylander Stage 49br; Carmen Sedano 110cra; Gordon Sinclair 77cl; Michael Sparrow 60br; Aleksandrs Tihonovs 50t; Ivan Vdovin 97cl; WWPicsz / Felipe Rodriguez 91br; Bax Walker 111cr; Ken Welsh 21cr, 70cl; Tony West 39cr; Tim E White 90cl; Wiskerke 54bl.

**Bridgeman Images:** 43br.

**Consejería de Turismo, Comercio y Deportes de la Junta de Andalucía:** 4t, 13cr, 17t, 24cl.

**Corbis:** EPA/ Julio Munez 91tl; the food passionates/ Hendrik Holler 76t; Owen Franken 76bc; Hemis/Patrick Escudero 4cla; Katja Kreder 42cr; Ocean/Marco Brivio 53crb.

**Dreamstime.com:** Adreslebedev 78tr; Alexsalcedo 79tr; David Acosta Allely 26clb; Amoklv 32clb; Angellodeco 72cla; Arenaphotouk 34cr, 35tc, 35crb, 38bl, 51crb, 100bc, 106clb; Artur Bogacki 24bc, 106tl; Boris Breytman 31tl; Paul Brighton 74cl; Gunold Brunbauer 4clb; Ryhor Bruyeu 69cl, Carpaumar 94tl, Sorin Colac 24cr; Shchipkova Elena 10crb, Serban Enache 10bl; Iakov Filimonov 7cra, 96br; Fotomicar 61cl; Jordi Clave Garsot 18cr; Grantotufo 96tl; Silvia Blaszczyszyn Jakiello 86cl; Lukasz Janyst 33tc; Jarcosa 95cr; Jesole 27tl; Kiko Jiménez 57tl, 86br; Joserpizarro 2tr, 40-1, 68t; Marcin Jucha 75tr; Karelgallas 60t; Vichaya Kiatying-angsulee 4crb, 21t, 86tl; Karol Kozlowski 12bl, 16cr, 59t, 104tl; Dmitry Kushch 44b; Emanuele Leoni 10cl, 14tl, 19l; Elisa Locci 26-7; Lotsostock 16tl; Lunamarina 4b, 65br; Dariya Maksimova 98cra; Mardym 78b; Enrico Mariotti 100tl; Brian Maudsley 25cr; minnystock 30-1, 117c; Elena Moiseeva 74br; Moskwa 105cl;; Juan Moyano 32-3, 58cl, 74tr, 119clb; Aitor Muñoz Muñoz 127cl; Carlos Neto 31bl; Pathastings 75cla; Sean Pavone 2tl, 3tl, 4cl, 8-9, 30cl, 82-3, 85tl, 108br, 114-5; Perseomedusa 6cra; Pigprox 45tl, 89cra; Yuan Ping 11tl; Ppy2010ha 75clb; Quintanilla 37crb; Rangpl 32br; Alvaro Trabazo Rivas 107cl; Fesus Robert 103tl; Paloma Rodriguez De Los Rios Ramirez 118tr; Rubenconpi 12cla; Sborisov 12-3, 19br; Jozef Sedmak 25tc, 49tl, 52b, 84tl, 88tl, 118cl; Sergeialyoshin 10-1; Iryna Soltyska 23bl, 33cr; Jose I. Soto 13clb, 15cr, 16br; Alena Stalmashonak 20r; Nick Stubbs 39tl, 64b; Jan Sučko 11cra; Titelio

10cla; Aleksandar Todorovic 20cl, 42b, 85br; Typhoonski 27bl, 73br; Txematrull 11br; Venemama 68br; Alvaro German Vilela 10clb; Yury 124cl; Natalia Zakharova 99tr; Vladimir Zhuravlev 71t; Zoom-zoom 45br.

**El Camborio:** 121tr.

**El Rinconcillo:** 92t.

**Getty Images:** Hulton Archive / Print Collector 43tl; DEA/C. SAPPA 96c; Moment 67cl; NIS/ Diego Lopez Alvarez 36-7; David Ramos 81cl; UIG/Editorial Education Images 36b; Universal Images Group / Sepia Times 55tc.

**Getty Images/iStock:** Uwe Moser 28–29.

**Ministerio de Agricultura, Alimentación y Medio Ambiente**

**Gabinete de la Ministra:** 11clb, 36cl; CENEAM - MMA/J.M. Reyero 36crb, 37tc.

**Museo Torre de la Calahorra:** 23cb.

**Real Alcázar de Sevilla:** 21clb.

**Robert Harding Picture Library:** age fotostock/Daniel Sanz 6br; J.D. Dallet 22cl; Anna Elias 126tr; Jose Fuste Raga 126b; Sylvain Grandadam 93clb; Jose Lucas 120cr; Guy Thouvenin 89bl; Ben Welsh 66bl

**Shutterstock.com:** Diego Grandi 1; Jose Carlos Serrano 66tl; Wirestock Creators 102cla.

**SuperStock:** Iberfoto 124tr.

**Real Club Valderrama:** 109tr.

## Cover

Front and spine: **Shutterstock.com:** Diego Grandi.

Back: **AWL Images:** Matteo Colombo crb, Stefano Politi Markovina cla; **Dreamstime. com:** Tatiana Bralnina tl; **iStockphoto.com:** SeanPavonePhoto tr; **Shutterstock.com:** Diego Grandi b.

## Pull Out Map Cover

**Shutterstock.com:** Diego Grandi.

All other images © Dorling Kindersley

For further information see:
www.dkimages.com

Penguin
Random
House

First edition 2004

First published in Great Britain by
Dorling Kindersley Limited
DK, One Embassy Gardens, 8 Viaduct
Gardens, London, SW11 7BW, UK

The authorised representative in the EEA is
Dorling Kindersley Verlag GmbH. Arnulfstr.
124, 80636 Munich, Germany

Published in the United States by
DK US, 1745 Broadway, 20th Floor, New
York, NY 10019, USA

Copyright © 2004, 2024 Dorling
Kindersley Limited

A Penguin Random House Company

23 24 25 26 10 9 8 7 6 5 4 3 2 1

A CIP catalogue record is available
from the British Library.

A catalogue record for this book is available
from the Library of Congress.

ISSN 1479-344X

ISBN 978-0-2416-6308-0

Printed and bound in Malaysia

www.dk.com

*As a guide to abbreviations in visitor information
blocks:* **Adm** = admission charge; **D** = dinner.

MIX
Paper | Supporting
responsible forestry
FSC™ C018179

This book was made with Forest
Stewardship Council™ certified
paper – one small step in DK's
commitment to a sustainable future.
**For more information go to
www.dk.com/our-green-pledge**

### 7 Attire

Female flamenco costumes usually feature elaborate ruffles, fringed scarves and hair accessories, such as roses. Dresses with long, flouncy trains are called *bata de cola* and require special training to dance in. Male dancers often wear a waistcoat and dress shirt with fitted trousers and boots.

### 8 Sevillanas

Sevillanas originated as the Seguidilla dance, which still exists in the Castile region today. In the 19th century this strident dance was infused with flamenco spirit and became a popular folk dance now prevalent at Andalucían festivals. Sevillanas has four parts and is danced in pairs, with passing turns and elaborate arm and hand movements, accompanied by the guitar, cajón, castanets and clapping rhythms.

### 9 Flamenco Legends

A few people who advanced the art include singers Camarón de la Isla, El Fillo and La Niña de los Peines; guitarist Paco de Lucía; and dancers La Macarrona and Carmen Amaya.

Camarón de la Isla and Tomatito

### 10 Performances

Flamenco can be enjoyed in a variety of venues, such as formal theatres, *tablaos* (upscale forums) and even rustic cave settings, where you'll find well-choreographed, professional performances. For something more spontaneous, head to a *peña* (cultural association dedicated to flamenco) or an intimate flamenco bar.

**TOP 10 FLAMENCO VENUES**

Performers at Tablao El Arenal

**1 Tablao El Arenal, Seville**
MAP L4 ▪ C/Rodo 7 ▪ www.tablaoelarenal.com
Come for the first-class performances.

**2 Peña La Bulería, Jerez**
MAP B5 ▪ C/Empedrada 20 ▪ 856 77 20 53
Club named after a fast flamenco style that originated in Jerez.

**3 Museo de Baile Flamenco**
MAP B5 ▪ www.museodelbaileflamenco.com
Shows staged in an intimate setting.

**4 Taberna Flamenca La Cava, Cádiz**
MAP B5 ▪ C/Antonio López 16, Cádizs ▪ flamencolacava.com
Enjoy flamenco in the setting of a traditional tavern.

**5 Puro Arte**
MAP B5 ▪ Calle Madre de Dios 10, Jerez de la Frontera ▪ 660 03 04 20
Book ahead to see acclaimed artists.

**6 Casa de la Memoria, Seville**
A museum, gallery and cultural centre with performances (see p91).

**7 Tablao Flamenco Cardenal, Córdoba**
MAP D3 ▪ C/Buen Pastor 2 ▪ www.tablaoflamencocardenal.es
Enjoy magical flamenco in an 18th-century manor.

**8 Venta El Gallo, Granada**
MAP F4 ▪ Barranco de los Negros 5 ▪ www.cuevaventaelgallo.es
Professional performances. Book early.

**9 La Peña Platería, Granada**
MAP F4 ▪ Placeta de Toqueros 7 ▪ www.laplateria.org.es
One of Spain's oldest *peñas*.

**10 La Canastera, Almería**
MAP G4 ▪ C/Cordoneros 5 ▪ 662 14 32 31 ▪ Performances 8pm Thu & Sat
Skilled amateurs dance flamenco.

# 🔟 Museums and Galleries

### ① Sala Antiquarium, Seville

MAP M2 ▪ Plaza de la Encarnación ▪ 955 47 15 80 ▪ Open 10am–8pm Tue–Sat, 10am–2pm Sun & public hols ▪ Adm

This subterranean museum, situated below the extraordinary Metropol Parasol structure in Plaza de la Encarnación, showcases the fascinating archaeological remains found in 1973 when the Parasol complex was being built. Extensive Roman ruins date from the Tiberius era onwards (around 30–600 CE) and there is a Moorish house dating back to the 12th–13th century.

### ② Museo de Bellas Artes, Seville

Housed in an exquisite former convent, this art museum (see p87) is second only to Madrid's famed Prado. Paintings include early works by Velázquez, and important pieces by Zurbarán, Ribera, El Greco, Murillo, Valdés Leal and Vásquez.

### ③ Museo Automovilistico y de la Moda, Málaga

Edificio de La Tabacalera, en Avenida Sor Teresa Prat 15 ▪ 951 13 70 01 ▪ Open 10am–2:30pm & 4–7pm daily ▪ Adm ▪ www.museoautomovilmalaga.com

This museum has an excellent private collection of classic cars, with models from automobile designers like Ettore Bugatti, Giuseppe Figoni, Firestone and Labourdette. There is also a section dedicated to haute couture.

**Exhibit at the Museo Automovilistico**

### ④ Museo Picasso, Málaga

This is the world's third-largest museum dedicated to the modern master, and honours Picasso's wish for his native city (see p104) to have a part of his artistic legacy. With over 187 paintings, including some major canvases, the collection here covers eight decades of the artist's career and gives an idea of the breadth and depth of Picasso's work.

### ⑤ Centre Pompidou, Málaga

MAP S5 ▪ Pasaje Doctor Carrillo Casaux ▪ 951 92 62 00 ▪ Open 9:30am–8pm Wed–Mon ▪ www.centrepompidou-malaga.eu

This offshoot of the renowned Parisian art museum has some unusual and thought-provoking pieces and features artists such as Francis Bacon, Frida Kahlo, René Magritte and Pablo Picasso. Exhibitions are divided and displayed as per themes.

**Museo de Bellas Artes, Seville**